A PRACTICAL GUIDE TO PERCUSSION TERMINOLOGY

RUSS GIRSBERGER

Edited and
with Performance Interpretation by
Anthony J. Cirone

A PRACTICAL GUIDE TO PERCUSSION TERMINOLOGY

RUSS GIRSBERGER

Edited and with
Performance Interpretation by
Anthony J. Cirone

cations
a division of G.W. Music, Inc.
170 N.E. 33rd St., Ft. Lauderdale, FL 33334

Meredith Music Publications and its stylized double M logo
are trademarks of Meredith Music Publications,
a division of G.W. Music, Inc.

Book and cover design by Shawn Brown

International Standard Book Number: 1-57463-059-8

Library of Congress Catalog Card Number: 98-67352

First Edition
September 1998

~ FOREWORD

The great orchestral compositions of the Classical and Romantic periods have transcended hundreds of years of interpretation by the world's greatest conductors and yet, these compositions continue to evolve with an endless stream of new ideas. Music notation is a very complicated system with a variety of dots, dashes, lines, and accents that help the composer communicate emotion in music. The interpretation of these markings keep music alive and refreshing.

Composers also rely on the written language to enhance musical notation. The words and phrases composers use are clues to a greater understanding of the meaning and character they wish to communicate. The tempo marking of *Allegro* may indicate the relative speed of a passage, but *Allegro maestoso* conveys a greater emotional meaning. Words are also used to give performance directives to musicians. Composers constantly embellish the musical notation with terms such as *dolce* and *agitato.*

As percussionists, we seem to generate more than our share of words to help explain the exact instrument required and the type of mallet necessary to create the desired sound. The fact that contemporary composers are continually inventing new sounds only increases the demand for more words.

The challenge of interpreting the written word in a musical score is complicated by the fact that most terms in the great Classical and Romantic compositions are written in foreign languages. The most common languages are Italian, German, and French (in that order). In my high school and college days these romance languages were quite fashionable among the student population, and little did I realize how important they would be in my musical career. Today, Spanish is the language of choice and although it is very beneficial in education and business, we see virtually no Spanish in musical compositions (with the exception of those by such Spanish-speaking composers as Manual de Falla and Alberto Ginastera).

Just as a musical phrase may be interpreted in a variety of ways, many foreign terms have taken on different meanings. I have always been amazed to listen to other orchestral percussion sections perform familiar repertoire quite differently than we would with the San Francisco Symphony. Many years ago, I attended a session on Ravel's *Daphnis et Chloé* presented by the Philadelphia Orchestra percussion section at a Percussive Arts Society convention. I could not believe my ears when I heard them play the famous part in the 2nd Suite written for *caisse claire* (snare drum) on a tenor drum. Immediately after the clinic I asked the section about this and was told that Eugene Ormandy, their Music Director for many years, specifically requested this part be performed on the tenor drum—end of discussion!

Every orchestra has similar traditions because of the experiences of the players and conductors. What we have tried to accomplish in this collection is to represent the terms in their most practical applications. When a term may be ambiguous, an interpretation is provided immediately following the description.

This *Practical Guide to Percussion Terminology* will be remarkably helpful to students, professionals, educators, conductors, and composers alike. Containing instruments, terms, and phrases, I feel it will serve as a significant resource for the study and performance of percussion music.

Thanks to Royal J. Hartigan for contributing to the list of West African instruments.

—Anthony J. Cirone

INTRODUCTION

This handbook is a practical guide to common terms found in orchestra, band, ensemble, and solo literature for percussion instruments. It should be considered as an aid to the working percussionist, conductor, composer, educator, and student searching to identify unfamiliar terms and instruments.

Because of the wide-ranging and international nature of percussion, it makes no attempt to identify all instruments and terms. Nor does it include musical terms common to all performers that can be found in general music dictionaries, or those descriptive phrases which do not directly relate to percussion instruments or their performance.

It does include instrument names, instructional phrases describing performing techniques or musical instructions, and descriptive terms in English, German, French, Italian, Spanish and occasionally other foreign languages.

Entries are arranged alphabetically. Direct translations are given following the language abbreviation. Longer definitions may include italicized words that serve as cross references to other entries. The comments on the practical interpretation of some terms by Anthony J. Cirone are indented from the definition and set in italics. A list of longer phrases found in the standard orchestral literature appears in the back of the book.

The following abbreviations identify the language of the term or phrase:

(Af.-Ewe)	African Ewe people	(Hun.)	Hungarian
(Af.-Akan)	African Akan people	(It.)	Italian
(Af.-Dag.)	African Dagomba people	(Lat.)	Latin
(Braz.)	Brazilian	(Pol.)	Polish
(Cze.)	Czechoslovakian	(Por.)	Portuguese
(Dan.)	Danish	(Rus.)	Russian
(Dut.)	Dutch	(Sp.)	Spanish
(Fr.)	French	(Swe.)	Swedish
(Ger.)	German		

A

à 2 (Fr.) by two; to be played by two players or by two instruments, such as a pair of *crash cymbals*

The most common use of this term for percussion instruments is with cymbal parts. Composers use "à2" to denote the use of crash cymbals. Wherever else it may be found, it would refer to the use of two players.

à deux (Fr.) by two; to be played by two players or by two instruments, such as a pair of *crash cymbals*
a due (It.) by two; to be played by two players or by two instruments, such as a pair of *crash cymbals*
a filo (Sp.) at the edge
à l'ordinaire (Fr.) ordinarily; as ordinarily played
à la jante (Fr.) on the rim
abämpfung (Ger.) remove mute
abdämpfen (Ger.) dampen; mute; *muffled*
abwechselnd (Ger.) alternating; played by turns
acciàio (It.) steel
acciarino (It.) triangle
accordato (It.) tuned to
accordé (Fr.) tuned to
acier (Fr.) steel
acme siren whistle brand name for a *siren whistle*
acme whistle brand name for a *pea whistle*
acuto (It.) sharp; high pitched
adjá (Braz.) cowbell used by Afro-Brazilian religious groups, similar to *agogo bells*
adufe small, hand-played *frame drum* found in Iberia, Portugal, and Brazil
aeolian bells *wind chimes* consisting of small bells, set in motion by touching or stroking of the hand
aeoliphon (Ger.) wind machine
aeoliphone wind machine

aerófono (It., Sp.) aerophone

aerophone an instrument made to sound by wind or air movement, such as a *whistle, siren, bull roarer,* or *pop gun*

afochê see *afuche*

afoxê Brazilian and Latin American rattle, similar to the *afuche*

African shakers small wicker shakers filled with seeds or pebbles

African slit drum see *slit drum*

African talking drum see *talking drum*

African thumb piano see *thumb piano*

Afrikanische harfe (Ger.) marimbula

Afrikanische schlitztrommel (Ger.) slit drum

Afro-Brazilian musical bow see *berimbau*

afuche gourd rattle from Brazil and Latin America. The gourd is surrounded by a net of beads which are shaken, struck, or rubbed against the gourd shell. The modern instrument has metal beads encircling a ribbed metal cylinder.

afuxé Brazilian rattle, similar to the *afuche* and *cabasa,* but with a coconut shell body, instead of a gourd

agitare (It.) to play in an agitated manner

agiter (Fr.) to play in an agitated manner

agitez (Fr.) to agitate, usually by shaking, rubbing, or stirring

agogo bells two conical-shaped bells of different sizes and pitches, connected by a U-shaped rod and struck with a beater. Made of either metal or wood, they are used in both Latin American and African music.

aigu (Fr.) high pitched; treble

aiguille à tricoter (Fr.) knitting needle

air-raid siren an *aerophone,* operated by hand crank or electric motor, which creates an ascending and descending *glissando*

akom dawuro (Af.-Akan) a long, flat, metal chamber which is open at one end. It is held in one hand and struck with a wooden stick as the opening is covered and uncovered to created muted and open tones.

al centro (It.) at the center

al cérchio (It.) on the hoop; on the rim

al màrgine (It.) at the edge

alarm bell a heavy cast *bell* of brass or bronze, struck by a interior clapper or with a mallet

àlbero di sonàgli (It.) bell tree

all'ordinario (It.) ordinarily; as ordinarily played

alla metà (It.) at the middle

alle (Ger.) all; tutti

allein (Ger.) alone; solo

allentare (It.) to slacken; to loosen

almglocken (Ger.) *cowbell* of the European Alps. They have a more rounded body than their American counterpart and are struck by an internal clapper, a stick, or a mallet. Tuned almglocken may be arranged in chromatic sets.

Alpenglocken (Ger.) almglocken

Alpine herd cowbells see *almglocken*

alto metallophone *bar percussion instrument* developed for use with Carl Orff's schulwerk music education program. This metal bar instrument has a diatonic or chromatic range from middle c to a above the treble clef staff.

alto xylophone *bar percussion instrument* developed for use with Carl Orff's schulwerk music education program. This wood bar instrument has a diatonic or chromatic range from middle c to a above the treble clef staff.

alto-soprano metallophone *bar percussion instrument* developed for use with Carl Orff's schulwerk music education program. This metal bar instrument has a diatonic or chromatic range from middle c to a above the treble clef staff, combining the range of the soprano and the alto metallophone.

alto-soprano xylophone *bar percussion instrument* developed for use with Carl Orff's schulwerk music education program. This wood bar instrument has a diatonic or chromatic range from middle c to a above the treble clef staff, combining the range of the soprano and the alto xylophone.

aluminophone *mallet percussion instrument* with aluminum *bars,* used in early recordings. It was a predecessor of the *vibraphone.*

aluminum harp a series of aluminum or nickel-plated tubes rubbed with rosined gloves which creates a sound similar to *musical glasses.* The instrument was manufactured by the J. C. Deagan Company.

am rand (Ger.) at the edge; at the rim

am rande der membrane (Ger.) at the edge of the head

am rande des felles (Ger.) at the edge of the head

ambira the name of two different African instruments: 1) a *xylophone* from Ethiopia with membranes on the *resonators,* similar to a *Mexican marimba*; 2) a *lamellaphone* of the *mbira* type.

ambose (Ger.) anvil

amboss (amboß) (Ger.) anvil

American Indian drum single or double-headed drum played by Native American Indian tribes. It has a wood or clay shell and thick skin heads held in place by leather straps. It is struck by wooden sticks or covered beaters as accompaniment to singing or dancing.

amortiguar (Sp.) to mute; to muffle; to choke

ancient cymbals small, thick, brass discs tuned to a definite pitch, struck together or with a hard beater. The instruments are available in a range of approximately two octaves and sound two octaves above the written pitch. Also known as *crotales* or *antique cymbals.*

anfangsgründe (Ger.) rudiments (of drumming)

angebunden (Ger.) fixed; attached

angklung tuned rattles of Java and Oceania. Each instrument has two or three bamboo tubes, pitched in octaves, which rest in a bamboo channel and are shaken back and forth.

animal bells any type of bell hung around the neck of an animal, made of wood, metal, or other materials. Examples include *almglocken* and *cowbells.*

animal sounds various types of animal calls and noises, created by imitative instruments, such as a *bird call, dog bark,* or *horse hooves.*

ankle bells small strung *rattles* or *pellet bells* worn around the ankles of dancers

anschlagen (Ger.) to strike; to beat

anschlagstellen (Ger.) striking position; beating spot

antiguos cimbalos (Sp.) antique cymbals

antik cymbeln (Ger.) antique cymbals

antike zimbeln (Ger.) antique cymbals

antique cymbals small, thick, brass discs tuned to a definite pitch, struck together or with a hard beater. The instruments are available in a range of approximately two octaves, and sound two octaves above the written pitch. Also known as *crotales* or *ancient cymbals.*

antiques cymbales (Fr.) antique cymbals

anvil a metal block or bar of indefinite pitch. Originally an actual blacksmith's anvil, substitute instruments include a *metal pipe, metal plate,* or a section of railroad rail.

apagar (Sp.) to mute; to muffle; to choke

apentemma (Af.-Akan) a medium-sized, single-headed drum carved from wood in a round, bowl-like shape. It may be played with sticks or hands.

apito (Por.) Brazilian whistle

appeau (Fr.) bird call

appéna toccata (It.) scarcely touching
Arabian hand drum see *darabucca*
arabische trommel (Ger.) Arabian drum. See *darabucca.*
arco (It.) to play with a *bow*
arenaiuolo (Ger.) sand rattle; maracas
armonica instrument consisting of *musical glasses* invented by Benjamin Franklin in 1761. Also known as a *glass harmonica.*
armonica de vetro (It.) glass harmonica
ärophon (Ger.) aerophone
arrêter (Fr.) to stop; to muffle
ass, jawbone of an see *jawbone of an ass*
assovious (Por.) whistle
atabal (Sp.) timpani
atabalero (Sp.) timpanist
atabaqué single-headed, barrel-shaped Brazilian drum, similar to the *conga drum.* The drum comes in three sizes: rum (largest), rumpí, and lê (smallest). They may be played with the hands, with sticks, or a combination of both.
atambor (Sp.) Arabian double-headed drum, often used in processional and military music
atoke (Af.-Ewe) a hollow, boat-shaped iron bell played with a long, thin metal rod
atsimeyu (Af.-Ewe) a master drum of the Ewe people, it is a tall, single-headed *barrel drum* with a deep tone
atumpan large, barrel-shaped, single-headed *talking drum* of Ghana, West Africa
au bord (Fr.) at the edge; at the rim
au bord de la membrane (Fr.) at the edge of the head
au centre (Fr.) at the center
au milieu (Fr.) at the middle
auf beiden fellen (Ger.) on both heads
auf dem fell (Ger.) on the skin
auf dem rand (Ger.) on the rim
auf dem reifen (Ger.) on the hoop
auf den saiten (Ger.) play with snares engaged
auf der kuppel (Ger.) on the bell of the cymbal
auf der mitte (Ger.) at the middle; at the center
aufgehängt (Ger.) hanging; suspended
auto horn air horn that imitates an early automobile horn or *taxi horn.* It is operated by squeezing a rubber bulb which forces air through the metal body, creating a loud honking sound.
autobremstrommeln (Ger.) brake drum

autohupe (Ger.) auto horn
automobile brake drum see *brake drum*
avec (Fr.) with
avec cordes (Fr.) with snares; play with snares engaged
avec deux mains (Fr.) with both hands
avec le bois (Fr.) with the wood
avec le pouce (Fr.) with the thumb; i.e., thumb roll
avec les cordes lâches (Fr.) with snares off
avec les doigts (Fr.) with the fingers
avec les mains (Fr.) with the hands
avec sourdine (Fr.) with mute; with damper
avec timbres (Fr.) with snares; play with snares engaged
axatse gourd *rattle* from Africa. The gourd is covered with a net of beads which are shaken and struck against the gourd shell.
ayacachtli gourd *rattle* of Mexico, often played in pairs

B

b.d. abbreviation for *bass drum*
bacchétta (It.) drum stick; mallet
bacchétta di fèrro (It.) iron rod or stick
bacchétta di gran cassa (It.) bass drum mallet
bacchétta di légno (It.) wooden stick
bacchétta di metallo (It.) metal stick
bacchétta di pèlle (It.) leather-headed stick
bacchétta di spugna (It.) sponge-headed stick
bacchétta di tamburo (It.) snare drum stick
bacchétta di tamburo militaire (It.) snare drum stick
bacchétta di timpani (It.) timpani stick
bacchétta di timpani a légno (It.) wooden timpani stick
bacchétta di timpani a spugna (It.) sponge-headed timpani stick
bacchétta di timpani mòlle (It.) soft-headed timpani stick
bacchétta di triàngolo (It.) triangle beater
bacchétta dura (It.) hard stick
bacchétta morbide (It.) soft stick
bacchétta ordinaria (It.) as ordinarily played
bacchétte del tamburo (It.) snare drum sticks
bacchétte di legno (It.) wood mallets
bacchétte di spunga (It.) sponge-headed mallets

bacchétte di vétro sospése (It.) glass wind chimes
bacchétto (It.) stick
back beat as heard in American popular music, emphasis placed on the unaccented beats in a measure. For rock or jazz music in 4/4 time, the second and fourth beats would be accented, usually by a heavy beat on the *snare drum, cymbal,* or other combination on the *drum set.*
backbone on skin *drum heads,* the area which laid against the animal's spine or backbone. Because this area is thicker and less responsive than the rest of the skin it is avoided as a playing area.
backsticking a method of turning the snare *drum stick* from its normal playing position to strike the *drum head* with the butt of the stick. Used in marching percussion sections for a visual effect.
baguette (Fr.) drum stick
baguette d'acier (Fr.) steel stick
baguette d'éponge (Fr.) sponge-headed stick
baguette de bois (Fr.) wooden stick
baguette de caisse claire (Fr.) snare drum stick
baguette de metal (Fr.) metal stick; metal beater
baguette de tambour (Fr.) snare drum stick
baguette de timbales (Fr.) timpani stick
baguette de timbales douce (Fr.) soft-headed timpani stick
baguette de timbales en bois (Fr.) wooden timpani stick
baguette de triangle (Fr.) triangle beater
baguette douce (Fr.) soft stick
baguette dure (Fr.) hard stick
baguette en cuir (Fr.) leather-headed stick
baguette en éponge (Fr.) sponge-headed stick
baguette en fer (Fr.) iron stick; iron beater
baguette en metal (Fr.) metal stick; metal beater
baguette en rotin (Fr.) rattan stick
baguette entrechouquée (Fr.) concussion stick
baguette mince (Fr.) thin drum stick
baguette normale (Fr.) normal or ordinary stick
baguette ordinaire (Fr.) normal or ordinary stick
baguettes de verre suspendues (Fr.) glass wind chimes
baguettes ordinaires (Fr.) normal or ordinary sticks
baguettes seules (Fr.) single sticking; to play with one hand
bajo (Sp.) bass
balafon gourd-resonated *xylophone* of West Africa
balais (Fr.) brush; wire brushes
balais métallique (Fr.) wire brushes

bambàgia (It.) cotton wool; i.e., padded drum stick
bamboo rattle see *angklung*
bamboo scraper a short length of hollow bamboo with notches carved in the body, scraped with a short rod, stick, or bamboo splinter. It is similar to the *güiro.*
bamboo shaker a hollow piece of bamboo filled with shot or seed and shaken by hand
bamboo wind chimes lengths of bamboo, suspended from a frame to clatter together
bambou (Fr.) bamboo
bambou Brésilien (Fr.) Brazilian bamboo shaker
bambou suspendue (Fr.) bamboo wind chimes
bamboula see *bambulá*
bambù (It.) bamboo
bambù Brasiliano (It.) Brazilian bamboo shaker
bambù sospéso (It.) bamboo wind chimes
bambulá single-headed drum, played with both hands, common to the French Antilles and Louisiana
bambus (Ger.) bamboo
bambusraspel (Ger.) bamboo scraper
bambusrohre (Ger.) bamboo wind chimes
bambustrommel (Ger.) boobams
banda turca (It.) Janissary music
banya *hand drum* from northern and central India, it is the lower pitched of a set of *tablā drums,* also known as the *duggī.* It has a metal shell with a single skin head held on with leather straps. A circular patch of black paste is affixed to the center of the head to help focus the pitch of the drum.
baqueta (Por., Sp.) snare drum stick
baquettes entrechoquées (Fr.) concussion sticks
bar percussion instruments generic term for *mallet percussion instruments,* such as the *xylophone, marimba, vibraphone,* and *orchestra bells*
baraban (Rus.) drum
baril de bois (Fr.) a wooden barrel, or barrel drum
baril de sake (Fr.) sake barrel
barile di legno (It.) a wooden barrel, or barrel drum
barile di sake (It.) sake barrel
barking dog see *dog bark*
barrel drum any drum with a barrel shape, i.e., with a larger diameter in the middle than at the ends

bars the tuned wood, metal, or synthetic keys of a *bar percussion instrument*

Basel drum rope-tensioned *field drum* used in rudimental music associated with the city of Basel, Switzerland

Basel drumming the rudimental style of snare drumming which originated in Swiss military music

basket rattle a container of woven bamboo or plant material which holds seeds or pellets

basketrommel see *tambour de basque*

Basle drum see *Basel drum*

Basler trommel (Ger.) Basel drum

basque trommel (Ger.) tambourine

bass drum a large drum of indefinite pitch, usually double-headed. The orchestral instrument is mounted vertically or horizontally on a stand and struck with a large beater. The bass drum of a *drum set* rests on the floor and is struck with a foot-operated beater.

bass drum pedal foot-operated beater used to strike a floor-mounted *bass drum*

bass drum pedal with cymbal striker a *bass drum pedal* with a metal arm attached to the shaft of the beater. In the early 20th century, it was used to strike a small cymbal that was attached to the hoop of a floor-mounted bass drum, while the bass drum beater simultaneously struck the head.

bass drum with attached cymbal a concert *bass drum* with a *crash cymbal* mounted upside down on the drum shell. The cymbal is clashed by its mate held in the player's left hand, while the bass drum is struck with a beater held in the right hand.

This technique is most commonly found in the symphonies of Gustav Mahler. Two other famous works are Pétrouchka *by Igor Stravinsky and 3 Pieces for Orchestra by Alban Berg. Mahler was creating the sound of German brass bands where one player played the bass drum and cymbals.*

Another version of this technique is where the bass drum is played with a foot pedal while the player uses a pair of crash cymbals. Ballet and theater orchestras may utilize this setup because of lack of space or for economic reasons.

bass metallophone bar percussion instrument developed for use with Carl Orff's schulwerk music education program. This metal bar instrument has a diatonic or chromatic range from c in the bass clef to f above middle c.

bass xylophone instrument with a lower range than the standard *xylophone*

basse de Flandres (Fr.) bumbass

basso (It.) low; bass

baßtrommel (Ger.) bass drum

batá double-headed hourglass drum used in Afro-Cuban music. The three sizes are iyá (largest, and the master drum), itótele, and okónkole or amelé (smallest). The drummer plays seated, striking the small head with the left hand and the large head with the right.

batería (Sp.) battery; percussion section

batintín (Sp.) Chinese gong

bâton (Fr.) drum stick; beater

bâton mince d'acier (Fr.) thin steel stick or beater

batte (Fr.) mallet; beater

battènte (It.) to beat, to hit, to strike; beater or stick

batter head the top head of a *snare drum*

batterìa (It.) battery; percussion section

batterie (Fr., It.) 1) battery; percussion section; 2) drum set

battery the percussion section of an orchestra, band, or other musical ensemble

battre (Fr.) to beat, to strike

battuto (It.) beaten, hammered, struck

batutto colla mano (It.) struck with the hands

baya *hand drum* from northern and central India, it is the lower pitched of a set of *tablā drums,* also known as the *duggī.* It has a metal shell with a single skin head held on with leather straps. A circular patch of black paste is affixed to the center of the head to help focus the pitch of the drum.

beaten rattles a family of percussion rattles which are sounded by striking or shaking, to include the *sistrum, spurs, angklung,* and *vibraslap*

beater mallet, stick, or striker used to create sound on percussion instruments

beben (Pol.) drum

becken (Ger.) cymbal(s)

becken an der grosse trommel befestigt (Ger.) cymbal attached to the bass drum. See *bass drum with attached cymbal.*

becken auf ständer (Ger.) cymbal on a stand; i.e., suspended cymbal

becken frei (Ger.) free cymbal; i.e., suspended cymbal
becken hängend (Ger.) hanging cymbal; i.e., suspended cymbal
becken mit fußmaschine (Ger.) hi-hat
becken mit teller (Ger.) crash cymbals
becken mit tellern (Ger.) crash cymbals
becken naturlich (Ger.) crash cymbals
becken paarweise (Ger.) pair of cymbals; crash cymbals
becken tambourin (Ger.) tambourine
beckenmaschine (Ger.) hi-hat
beckenriemen (Ger.) cymbal strap
beckenschlag (Ger.) cymbal crash
beckentrommel (Ger.) tambourine without a head
bedeckt (Ger.) covered (with)
bedug large, double-headed, barrel-shaped drum used in the Javanese *gamelan* orchestra. The drum is suspended from a frame and struck with a mallet.
befestigt (Ger.) fastened; attached
beffroi (Fr.) alarm bell
beinklapper (Ger.) clappers; bones
belegt (Ger.) covered; *muffled*
bell brass, bronze, or cast percussion instrument, hollow and struck to ring by an internal clapper. They are constructed in a variety of sizes, to include *church bells, dinner bells,* and *hand bells.*
bell chimes a set of small, tuned, suspended bells, usually without clappers, which are struck with a mallet or hammer
bell clapper a striker or beater hung inside a *bell* which strikes the instrument when the bell is swung or shaken
bell lyra a portable *glockenspiel* used in marching bands, with steel or aluminum *bars* set in a frame in the shape of a music lyre. The instrument is held vertically, supported in a harness and by one hand, while the bars are struck with a mallet held in the other hand. The instrument sounds two octaves above the written pitch.
bell (of cymbal) the raised area in the center of a *cymbal*
bell piano a specially constructed string instrument, resembling a large dulcimer, used to simulate the sound of bells in Wagner's *Parsifal*
bell plate a thick, rectangular metal plate, suspended by rope, and struck with a hard beater. The bronze or steel plate may be of indefinite pitch or tuned.
bell strap *ankle bells* worn by Native American dancers

bell tree a series of cup-shaped bells, suspended on a string or pole, arranged by size from the largest (lowest pitched) to the smallest. They are played with a brass or metal striker in a *glissando* from one end to the other.
bells generic term for *orchestra bells* or *glockenspiel*
bells of wood see *wood bell*
bendir a north African *frame drum* with *snares* underneath its single head
berimbau a musical bow from Brazil. A single wire connects the top and bottom of a bowed stick held in the left hand. A gourd *resonator* at the bottom of the bow is held by the stomach to control resonance. The wire is struck by a smaller stick in the right hand, which also holds a small wicker shaker. A coin pressed against the wire changes the pitch of the struck wire.
besen (Ger.) wire brushes
bicchièri di vétro (It.) tuned glasses
big drum bass drum
bin-sasara a series of small boards, strung in a row on a rope, with a handle on each end. When the handle is shaken it creates a rippling effect, producing a rattling noise, similar to a *rachet.*
bird call an imitative call, *whistle,* or mechanical effect used to replicate bird song or sounds
bird whistle a *whistle,* blown to imitate bird song or sounds
birimbau see *berimbau*
bis zur unhörbarkeit abnehmen (Ger.) diminish to where the sound is almost inaudible
bladder and strings English name for the *bumbass*
blechtrommel (Ger.) steel drum
bloc chinois (Fr.) Chinese block, temple block
bloc de bois (Fr.) wood block
bloc de bois cylindrique (Fr.) cylindrical wood block
bloc de métal (Fr.) anvil; cowbell
bloc en bois (Fr.) wood block
bloc métallique (Fr.) metal block
blòcchi di légno coreano (It.) Korean wood block; temple block
blòcco di légno (It.) wood block
blòcco di légno Cinese (It.) Chinese wood block; temple block
blòcco di légno coreano (It.) Korean wood block; temple block
blòcco di metallo (It.) anvil; cowbell
blocs a papier di verre (Fr.) sandpaper blocks
bloque de madera (Sp.) wood block
bloque de metal (Sp.) anvil; cowbell

board clapper see *slapstick*
boat whistle a *whistle* or mechanical effect used to imitate boat, steamship, or battleship whistles and horns
bodhrán single-headed *frame drum* of Ireland. The instrument is held by an x-shaped frame and struck with a small, wooden, two-headed beater.
bois (Fr.) wood
boite en bois (Fr.) wood block
bomb a loud, unexpected accent played on the *bass drum*, heard in bebop style jazz drumming
bombo (Sp.) bass drum
bonang tuned gong of the Javanese *gamelan* orchestra
bones a pair of small, slightly curved wooden sticks, held between the fingers and clicked together by a quick flick of the wrist. They produce a sound similar to *castanets.*
bonghi (It.) bongo drums
bongo drums a pair of small, single-headed drums common to Latin American music. The drums are usually struck with the fingers and held between the legs or mounted on a stand.
bongos see *bongo drums*
bongotrommel (Ger.) bongo drums
boobams small, single-headed tuned drums, played with fingers, sticks, or mallets. The narrow drums have long shells made of bamboo or plastic, with heads of skin or plastic. The length of the shell and the head tension determines the pitch of the drum; diatonic or chromatic sets are common.
bord (Fr.) edge; rim
borde (Sp.) edge; rim
bórdo (It.) edge; rim
bordón (Sp.) snare
boss the raised center area on a *gong* or *cymbal*
bosun's pipe high-pitched metal *whistle* used for communication aboard ship
bottles, tuned see *tuned bottles*
bourdon (Fr.) pasteboard rattle or waldteufel
bouteillophone (Fr.) tuned bottles
bow an instruction to draw the bow of a string instrument across a percussion instrument to create a sustained tone.

To draw the bow of a violin, viola, cello or bass across the body of a percussion instrument. The most effective instruments that can be "bowed" include crotales, suspended cymbal, gong, and vibraphone. It is also possible to "bow" other bar percussion instruments (glockenspiel, xylophone, and marimba). Use a violin or viola bow on crotales and suspended cymbal and the larger cello and bass bows on the gong and vibraphone.

bowl the body or kettle-shaped resonating cavity of *timpani*, usually made from copper, metal alloy, or fiberglass

brake drum the metal housing from an automobile brake assembly. When struck by wood or metal beaters it rings with an pitched metallic tone, similar to an *anvil.*

Brake drums may be muted or suspended. To mute a brake drum, simply place it on a padded surface, open side down, and play on the body with hard rubber mallets. Suspended brake drums may be mounted on a frame or inverted on a padded surface with the open side facing up. Strike the drum on the outside edge.

brass hammers mallets with a small brass ball on the end, usually used on metal bar *orchestra bells* or a *bell tree*

Brazilian bamboo shaker see *bamboo shaker*

bremstrommeln von autos (Ger.) brake drum

brettchenklapper (Ger.) slapstick; clappers; bones

bronze bell a large, suspended, cast *bell* sounded by an internal striker

bronze drum a metal drum from Indonesia and Asia with its shell and single head made of bronze. Also known as a frog drum for the decorative frogs on some drum shells.

brosse (Fr.) wire brushes

bruit de sonnaille des troupeaux (Fr.) cowbell

bruit de tôle (Fr.) foil rattle

brummeisen (Ger.) Jew's harp

brummtopf (Ger.) friction drum; lion's roar

brushes see *wire brushes*

bubbolo (It.) jingles; pellet bells

buben (Cze.) drum

bubénchik (Rus.) pellet bells; sleigh bells

buckelgong (Ger.) button gong

bulb horn air horn operated by squeezing a rubber bulb which forces air through the metal body to create a loud honking sound

bull roarer a flat blade of wood, bone, or stone, with a length of string tied to one end. The blade is swung through the air over the player's head to make a whirring roar.

bumbass a one-man-band instrument consisting of a tall stick with a pair of *cymbals* on top, a single-string running across a small *drum* near the bottom, and *pellet bells* attached at various points on the stick

Burma bell see *kyeezee*

Burton grip a manner of holding four mallets to facilitate playing multiple notes on *mallet percussion instruments*

butt end of stick the back, or thick end of a *drum stick*

buttibu (It.) friction drum

button gong any *gong* with a raised *boss* in the center which allows it to be tuned to a specific pitch. They are common in Indonesian *gamelan* orchestras.

buzz marimba see *Mexican marimba*

buzz roll see *closed roll*

C

cabaca see *cabasa*

cabaquinha square *frame drum* from Latin America

cabasa *gourd rattle* from Brazil and Latin America. Surrounding the gourd is a net of beads that is struck, shaken, and rubbed against the gourd shell. The commercial instrument has metal beads encircling a ribbed metal cylinder.

cabaza see *cabasa*

cabeza (Sp.) head; drum head

cable timpani *timpani* with a unique hand-tuning device. Sprockets on each tuning lug are connected by a cable which runs around the circumference of the drum. By turning one tuning lug, all lugs are turned simultaneously to change the pitch of the drum.

caccavella (It.) friction drum

cadenas (Sp.) chains

cadence percussion pattern used by marching percussion sections to keep troops and bands in step on the march. Usually written in even numbers of measures, they are repeated indefinitely until the journey or parade is completed.

cadre du tambour (Fr.) drum shell

caisse (Fr.) drum

caisse à timbre (Fr.) snare drum

caisse claire (Fr.) snare drum
caisse claire détimbrée (Fr.) snare drum with snares off
caisse claire grande taille (Fr.) large snare drum
caisse claire petite taille (Fr.) small snare drum
caisse plate (Fr.) piccolo snare drum
caisse roulante (Fr.) tenor drum
caisse roulante avec cordes (Fr.) field drum or parade drum
caisse sourde (Fr.) tom tom
caixa (Por.) snare drum
caixa clara (Por.) snare drum
caixa de rufo (Por.) tenor drum
caixeta (Por.) wood block
caja (Sp.) drum; specifically a double-headed drum, often with a *snare,* found in Spain, Cuba, and South America
caja china (Sp.) Chinese wood blocks
caja clara (Sp.) snare drum
caja rodante (Sp.) tenor drum
calabaza (Sp.) cabasa
calebasse (Fr.) cabasa
calf skin head a *drum head* made from the skin of a calf

Before the invention of the plastic head during the late 1950s, all drums used animal skins—usually calf skin. Calf skin heads are still popular with many players and are very effective on timpani, bass drum, snare drum, tom tom, and tambourines.

Calf skin heads need constant care to preserve enough collar between the head and shell. A good rule to remember is to "maintain the condition of the head in the opposite manner needed for performance." For example, a bass drum head must be loosened to produce a low, mellow tone, therefore tighten the head between rehearsals and performance so enough collar will remain to loosen it to the desired pitch. The reverse is true for the snare drum.

calottes (Fr.) small bells in the shape of a semi-circle, common to the Middle Ages
calung renteng *xylophone* made from bamboo tubes, found in Java and Indonesia
calypsotrommel (Ger.) steel drum
cambia in (It.) change to; used in *timpani* music to notate a change of pitch
cambiare l'accordatura (It.) to change the tuning; to retune

camel bells a series of cylindrical or conical metal *bells,* graduated in size and suspended by a string inside one another, which are struck or shaken
camesa see *kamesa*
campainha (Por.) bell
campana (It., Sp.) bell; chimes
campana d'allarme (It.) alarm bell
campana da preghièra (It.) prayer bell; dobači
campana de mano (Sp.) hand bell
campana di légno (It.) wood block
campana grave (It.) low-pitched bell; church bell
campana in lastra di metallo (It.) bell plate
campana tubolari (It.) tubular bells; chimes
campanàccio (It.) cowbell
campanàccio di metallo (It.) cowbell
campanas tubulare (Sp.) tubular bells; chimes
campane (It.) bells; chimes
campane da gregge (It.) cowbell
campane da pastore (It.) herd bells
campane tubolare (It.) tubular bells; chimes
campanèlla (It.) small bell; orchestra bells
campanelle (It.) orchestra bells
campanelle de vacca (It.) cowbells
campanelli (It.) glockenspiel; orchestra bells
campanelli a tastièra (It.) keyboard glockenspiel
campanelli giapponése (It.) metal bar instrument with *resonators,* used by Puccini and others to simulate a Japanese instrument
campanello (It.) hand bell
campanello d'allarme (It.) alarm bell; ship's bell
campani (It.) chimes
campanilla (It.) hand bell
campano (Sp.) cowbell
campanólogo (Sp.) chimes; bells
caña (Sp.) cane; rattan
canna (It.) cane; rattan
canne (Fr.) cane; rattan
cannon shot the sound made by the firing of a cannon, often simulated by striking a large *bass drum* in the center of the head
cannóne (It.) cannon; gun
canon (Fr.) cannon; gun
canusao (Por.) snare drum
caoutchouc (Fr.) rubber

capello cinese (It.) Turkish crescent
capoc (Fr.) see *kapoc*
car horn air horn that imitates an early automobile horn. It is operated by squeezing a rubber bulb which forces air through the metal body, creating a loud honking sound.
cara anterior (Sp.) batter head
cara con bordones (Sp.) snare head
caracacha Brazilian *bamboo scraper*
caracaxá Brazilian *bamboo scraper*
caraxa South American *scraper*
cariglione (It.) carillon bells; chimes
carillon (It.) orchestra bells
carillon bells a set of large bells operated from a manual or electronic keyboard console, intended for outdoor music and often placed in large towers. The typical substitute is *chimes.*
carraca (Sp.) ratchet
carrilhão (Por.) orchestra bells; glockenspiel
carta sabbiata (It.) sandpaper; sandpaper blocks
carta vetrata (It.) sandpaper; sandpaper blocks
cascabels (Sp.) jingle bells; sleigh bells; pellet bells
cascavels (Sp.) jingle bells; sleigh bells; pellet bells
cassa (It.) drum
cassa chiara (It.) snare drum
cassa del tamburo (It.) drum shell
cassa di legno (It.) wood block
cassa di metallo (It.) metal block
cassa grande (It.) bass drum
cassa rullante (It.) tenor drum
cassa sola (It.) bass drum to play solo, without accompanying cymbal
casse chiare (It.) snare drum
cassettina (It.) wood block
cassettina di legno (It.) wood block
cast bell see *bell*
castagnetta (It.) castanets
castagnette (It.) castanets
castagnette di fèrro (It.) metal castanets; mounted finger cymbals
castagnette di metallo (It.) metal castanets
castagnettes (Fr.) castanets
castagnettes à manche (Fr.) paddle castanets
castagnettes de fer (Fr.) metal castanets; mounted finger cymbals
castagnettes de métal (Fr.) metal castanets

castagnettes en bois et en fer (Fr.) wood and metal castanets
castagnettes sur socle (Fr.) castanet machine
castanet machine a pair of *castanets* mounted on a board and held apart by elastic or springs, so they may be struck together using fingers or soft mallets
castañeta (Sp.) castanets
castanets a pair of spoon-shaped wooden *clappers* attached by string, held with the fingers and clicked together. Castanets used in concert music are usually attached to a handle or separated by a central board and struck against the hand or leg.
castanhetas (Por.) castanets
castañuelas (Sp.) castanets
castañuelas de metal (Sp.) metal castanets
catacá (Braz.) scraper
caténa (It.) chains
catuba (It.) bass drum
caxambu large, single-headed wooden drum from Brazil, made from a hollow tree trunk
caxixi small wicker basket rattle from Brazil, used when playing the *berimbau*
celesta a keyboard instrument with steel bars struck by a piano action device. The range is generally five octaves and the instrument sounds one octave above the written pitch.
celeste see *celesta*
cencerro (Sp.) cowbell
ceppi cinése (It.) Chinese blocks; temple blocks
ceppi di carta vetrata (It.) sandpaper blocks
cérchio (It.) counter hoop; rim
cérchio della pèlle (It.) flesh hoop
cercle (Fr.) counter hoop, rim
chain timpani *timpani* with sprockets on each tuning lug which are connected by a chain that runs around the circumference of the drum. By turning one lug, all are tuned simultaneously to change the pitch of the drum.
chaînes (Fr.) chains
chains lengths of linked iron chain which are shaken or rattled
changez en (Fr.) change to; used in *timpani* music to notate a change of pitch
changgo double-headed hourglass-shaped drum from Korea
chapa de trueno (Sp.) thunder sheet
chapeau chinois (Fr.) Turkish crescent; bell tree
charleston beckenmaschine (Ger.) hi-hat

charleston cymbals a predecessor of the modern *hi-hat*
charlestonmaschine (Ger.) hi-hat
chekeré see *shekere*
chiaro (It.) clearly; to play in a clear manner
chimes metal tubes of bronze or brass arranged chromatically, typically one and one-half octaves in range and sounding at written pitch. They often substitute for church or *cast bells* or *carillon bells.* Struck with rawhide or plastic hammers, they may be dampened by a pedal operated mechanism. Also known as *tubular bells.*
China cymbal see *Chinese cymbal*
Chinese bell tree see *bell tree*
Chinese block wood block; temple block
Chinese Confucian bells small, bowl-shaped bells tuned in microtones. Also known as *dharma bells.*
Chinese crescent see *Turkish crescent*
Chinese cymbal a *cymbal* with a square bell and an upturned edge, intended to sound similar to a small *tam-tam*
Chinese drum a small drum with pigskin heads tacked onto the wood shell, often used on early *drum sets*
Chinese paper drum a small two-headed drum, with paper heads, mounted on a stick. As the stick is rotated back and forth, small balls tied to the shell swing and strike the heads.
Chinese pavilion see *Turkish crescent*
Chinese temple blocks see *temple blocks*
Chinese tom tom a small drum with pigskin heads tacked onto the wood shell, often used on early *drum sets*
Chinese wood blocks small slit drums; temple blocks
Chinesische becken (Ger.) Chinese cymbal
Chinesische blocke (Ger.) wood block; temple block
Chinesische tom tom (Ger.) Chinese tom tom
Chinesische zimbel (Ger.) Chinese cymbal
ching-a-ring a thin metal *tambourine* that is attached to the shaft of a *hi-hat* above the cymbals. It jingles when struck or shaken as a result of stepping on the hi-hat. It is also known as a ching ring.
chocalho metal shaker filled with shot or lead pellets, common to Latin American music
chocolo (Ger.) chocalho
choke to mute quickly, silencing the instrument's sound immediately. A technique often applied to the *cymbal.*
choke cymbal a thin, small diameter *cymbal* that is struck and quickly muffled to create staccato rhythmic patterns. It is used often in a jazz *drum set.*

choke cymbals hi-hat
church bell a large cast *bell* struck by an internal striker. *Chimes* are often used as a substitute.
cimbali (It.) cymbals
cimbali antichi (It.) antique cymbals
cimbalillos digitales (Sp.) finger cymbals
cimbalini (It.) antique cymbals; finger cymbals
címbalo (Sp.) cymbal
cìmbalo (It.) cymbal
címbalo antiguo (Sp.) antique cymbals
címbalo suspenso (Sp.) suspended cymbal
cimbalom a type of zither or dulcimer with tuned strings, struck by padded wooden sticks held in the fingers
címbalos dedos (Sp.) finger cymbals
cinellen (Ger.) cymbals
cinelli (It.) cymbal
cinelli dito (It.) finger cymbals
clacson (It.) klaxon
clapper the metal or wood striker found inside a *bell*
clappers pieces of wood, bone, or other material which are struck or slapped together to make a loud clapping sound. Examples include the *slapstick* and *concussion sticks.*
claquebois (Fr.) early name for the *xylophone*
claquette (Fr.) clapper; slapstick; rattle
clash cymbals crash cymbals
clashed cymbals crash cymbals
claves two cylindrical hardwood (often rosewood) sticks which are struck together. They are traditionally used in Latin American music, where they often play the rhythmic figure known as the clavé.
claxon see *klaxon*
clay rattles *rattles* or *maracas* made from clay
cliquette (Fr.) clappers
cloche (Fr.) bell; chimes
cloche à vache (Fr.) cowbell
cloche de vache (Fr.) cowbell
cloche en lame de métal (Fr.) metal plate; bell plate
cloches plaque (Fr.) bell plate
cloches tubulaire (Fr.) tubular bells; chimes
clochette (Fr.) small bell; hand bell
clochettes (Fr.) orchestra bells
clochettes à mains (Fr.) hand bells

clog box wood block

closed hi-hat *1) hi-hat* cymbals closed together by depressing the instrument's foot pedal; 2) to strike on closed hi-hat cymbals

closed roll a method of sustaining sound on a drum by bouncing the sticks on the head in rapid succession, with a minimum of three strokes from each stick. It is one of the standard drum *rudiments.*

A snare drum roll in orchestral or band music is referred to as a closed roll. However, the roll may be played open (fewer bounces) depending on the dynamics and character of the music. Drum corps use a "rudimental roll" consisting of two bounces for each stroke. Drum set players use the term "buzz roll" or "press roll" which is a tighter sounding roll (more bounces) than a closed roll.

closed stroke a stroke used on *hand drums* and *frame drums,* in which the fingers remain on the head after the stroke to muffle the sound

cloutée (Fr.) sizzle cymbal

clutch the device consisting of a tubular screw thread, felt pads, and lock washers, which holds the top *hi-hat* cymbal in position

cocktail drum a small *drum set* consisting of a deep and narrow *tom tom* on legs, sometimes with a small *cymbal* attached. The bottom head is struck by a *bass drum pedal* while the top head is struck with *drum sticks* or *wire brushes.*

coco South American wood block

coconut shells the two halves of a hollowed-out coconut shell, struck against a hard surface to imitate the sound of horse hoof beats

cog rattle a type of small *ratchet,* usually spun in the air by its handle

coil spring the metal suspension spring from an automobile, which rings with a resonant tone when struck with a metal beater

col (It.) with

col fèrro (It.) with metal

col légno (It.) with the wood

col mazza (It.) with a large mallet

col pollice (It.) with the thumb; i.e., thumb roll

Colgrass drums *tom tom* with a cardboard shell and wing nuts for tuning lugs. A predecessor of the *roto-tom,* it was developed by American composer Michael Colgrass.

colla (It.) with
colla mano (It.) with the hands or fingers
con (It.) with
con còrda (It.) with snares
con sordina (It.) with mute; *muffled*
concert music in this dictionary the term refers to music written for or played by an orchestra, band, or percussion ensemble in a concert performance setting
concert tom toms single-headed, tunable *tom toms* of varying depths and diameters, usually mounted on an upright stand for concert playing
concussion blocks two hardwood boards which are struck together, used in Japanese and Chinese theater music. Also known as *hyōshigi.*
concussion sticks a pair of small sticks which are struck against each other or against the ground
conga drum a deep, single-headed, barrel-shaped drum common to Cuban and Latin American music. The skin heads are struck with the hands and fingers. The three sizes are the quinto (smallest), conga, and tumba (largest).
conga trommel (Ger.) conga drum
conical drum a drum with a tapered shell in the shape of a cone
contre le genou (Fr.) strike against the knee
coperti (It.) covered, muted; *muffled*; also snares off
copèrto (It.) covered; muted; *muffled*; also snares off
coprire (It.) dampened; *muffled*; also snares off
coque de noix (Fr.) coconut shells
coquilles noix de coco (Fr.) coconut shells
cor d'auto (Fr.) auto horn
còrda (It.) strings; snares
cordes (Fr.) strings; snares
còrdes (It.) snares
coreani (It.) Korean blocks; temple blocks
corno di automobile (It.) auto horn
coucou (Fr.) cuckoo bird call
counter hoop a hoop of metal or wood which presses down on the *flesh hoop* and puts tension on the *drum head* by stretching it over the edge of the *drum shell*
coup (Fr.) stroke, as in a *drum stroke*
coup de bouchon (Fr.) pop gun
coup de charge a drum stroke in French and Swiss drumming styles

coup de marteau (Fr.) hammer stroke
coup de pistolet (Fr.) pistol shot
coup de revolver (Fr.) pistol shot
coups de verre (Fr.) tuned glasses
couvert (Fr.) covered; muted; *muffled*
covered muted; dampened; *muffled*
cowbell conical metal bell similar to those suspended from the necks of cows or herd animals. *Herd bells* have internal clappers, while the other instruments do not and must be struck by a stick or mallet to sound its tone.
crash cymbal in a *drum set,* a thin *suspended cymbal* with a rapid decay, used for accents
crash cymbal roll a sustained sound on *hand cymbals,* created by rapid strokes of both cymbals against each other
crash cymbals in concert music, a pair of *cymbals* held in each hand by straps and clashed together
crécelle (Fr.) rattle; ratchet
crescent see *Turkish crescent*
cross-sticking technique of playing where one hand crosses over the other to facilitate sticking on adjacent instruments
crotales small, thick, brass discs of definite pitch, struck together or with a hard beater. The instruments are available in a range of approximately two octaves, and sound two octaves above the written pitch. Also known as *ancient cymbals* or *antique cymbals.*
crotali (It.) crotales
crotalos (Sp.) crotales
crow call a bird call used to imitate a crow's caw
crown (of cymbal) see *bell (of cymbal)*
crystallophone a generic term for tuned *bar percussion instruments* made of glass sounded by striking or rubbing. Examples include the *armonica, glass harmonica,* and *musical glasses.*
csapás (Hun.) percussion
Cuban sticks see *claves*
Cuban tom toms see *bongo drums*
cuckoo bird call a *bird call* that imitates the sound of a cuckoo bird
cuculo (It.) cuckoo bird call
cuerdos de tripa (Sp.) gut snares
cuerno de auto (Sp.) auto horn
cuíca Brazilian *friction drum* with a bamboo stick tied to the underside of its single head. The stick is rubbed with a rosined or moistened cloth which causes the head to vibrate.

cuir (Fr.) leather; hide
cùpola (It.) bell of a cymbal
cyclone whistle see *siren whistle*
cylindrical drum a drum with a shell in the shape of a tapered cylinder
cylindrical wood block a tubular *wood block* with slits in either end, making it capable of two tones
cymbal round metal alloy disc of indefinite pitch. Their shape is gently curved with a raised *bell* or dome in the center. They can vary widely in diameter and thickness, each of which affects the tone. They are played singly, as a *suspended cymbal* struck by a stick or mallet, or in pairs as clashed *hand cymbals.*

The following foreign words: (Ger.) "becken," (It.) "piatti" or "cinelli," and (Fr.) "cymbales," all serve as generic terms for cymbals. None of these terms specifically refer to crash or suspended cymbals. Composers need to indicate whether they want crash cymbals (à2) or suspended cymbals (with stick). Composers also need to indicate what type of stick or mallet to use on the suspended cymbal, for example: yarn, wood, metal, wire brush, etc.

In much of the standard orchestral literature, composers did not provide enough information regarding the type of cymbal or the type of mallet. The players (and to a lesser degree, conductors) usually will make these decisions.

cymbal striker a metal arm attached to the shaft of a *bass drum pedal.* In the early 20th century, it was used to strike a small *cymbal* that was attached to the hoop of a floor-mounted *bass drum,* while the bass drum beater simultaneously struck the head.
cymbal tongs *finger cymbals* mounted on spring tongs which are squeezed to strike the cymbals together. Also known as *metal castanets.*
cymbale (Fr.) cymbal
cymbale charleston à pédale (Fr.) hi-hat
cymbale Chinoise (Fr.) Chinese cymbal
cymbale dedos (Sp.) finger cymbals
cymbale doigte (Fr.) finger cymbals
cymbale fixée à la grosse caisse (Fr.) bass drum with attached cymbal
cymbale libre (Fr.) suspended cymbal
cymbale suspendue (Fr.) suspended cymbal
cymbales à 2 (Fr.) crash cymbals

cymbales à l'ordinaire (Fr.) crash cymbals
cymbales à pédale (Fr.) hi-hat
cymbales antiques (Fr.) antique cymbals
cymbales choquées (Fr.) cymbals clashed together; crash cymbals
cymbales digitales (Fr.) finger cymbals
cymbalier (Fr.) cymbalist; cymbal player
cymbeln antik (Ger.) antique cymbals

D

d'acciàio (It.) steel
d'acier (Fr.) steel
d'éponge (Fr.) sponge
dabachi see *dobači*
dada-mama roll see *mama-dada roll*
dadaiko large *barrel drum* suspended in a wood frame and struck with padded beaters. It accompanies the dance in Japanese gagaku court music.
daf *frame drum* of the Middle East, Turkey, and Iran
dagga see *duggī*
dāhinā the higher-pitched of a set of *tabla drums,* which sits to the player's right. Also known as *tablā.*
daiko Japanese term for drum. It is used in compound words to identify specific instruments, such as *ōdaiko* and *dadaiko.*
daire large *frame drum* from south-eastern Europe and south and central Asia
daishōko large bronze *gong* used in Japanese gagaku court music
damaru wooden hourglass drum from India and Mongolia
dampen to muffle or mute the sound of the instrument
dämpfen (Ger.) muted; *muffled*; also snares off
dämpfer (Ger.) mute; muffler
dance drum *frame drum* used by musicians or participants as an accompaniment to the dance in many cultures
dance drums see *drum set*
daph *frame drum* from South Asia
dar con (Sp.) to hit; to strike
darabucca single-headed *goblet drum,* made from wood, pottery, or metal, from the Middle East and North Africa. It is held under the arm and struck with fingers and hands.

darabuka (Ger., Sp.) darabucca
darabukke (It.) darabucca
darboukka (Fr.) darabucca
darbuka (Sp.) darabucca
daula a double-headed drum from Sri Lanka, similar to the *davul*
daumen (Ger.) thumb
davul a large double-headed drum from Turkey. It is struck by a wooden beater on one head and a switch or cane on the other and is occasionally heard as a solo instrument.
dead stroke a stroke, often to the center of the *drum head,* which gives a short, muffled tone
découvert (Fr.) uncovered; open; i.e., not muted
dejar vibrar (Sp.) let vibrate; let ring
derabucca see *darabucca*
derbouka (Fr.) darabucca
derbuka (Ger.) darabucca
détendre (Fr.) to slacken; to loosen
devil's violin see *bumbass*
dharma bells small, bowl-shaped bells tuned in microtones. Also known as *Chinese Confucian bells.*
dhol double-headed *cylindrical drum* of Armenia
ḍhol generic term for several types of large *cylindrical drums* or *barrel drums* of South Asia
ḍholak generic term for several types of large *cylindrical drums* or *barrel drums* of South Asia, distinct however from the *ḍhol*
diable de bois (Fr.) pasteboard rattle or waldteufel
diavolo di bosco (It.) pasteboard rattle or waldteufel
diddle a double stroke with both notes played by the same stick, used in *rudimental drumming*
dinner bell small *bell* with a handle and an internal clapper, similar to a *hand bell*
dinner chimes a small, hand held set of three to six metal bars with *resonators*
dito (It.) finger
dito pollice (It.) thumb
djembe (Fr.) jembe
dob (Hun.) drum
dobači Japanese brass or bronze cup-shaped bell which rests on a small cushion
dog bark small *friction drum* with a string tied to its single head. A rosined rag is pulled along the string which causes the head to vibrate, imitating the bark of a dog.

doigt (Fr.) finger
doira *frame drum* of Eastern Europe
dolak see *ḍholak*
domed gong see *button gong*
donnerblech (Ger.) thunder sheet
donnermaschine (Ger.) thunder sheet
donno see *talking drum*
doppelkonustrommel (Ger.) double conical drum
doppelschlag (Ger.) double-headed beater
doppelter vorschlag (Ger.) drag
dora small, brass Japanese *button gong*
double bass the use of two bass drums in a *drum set*
double bell two metal bells of slightly different sizes (and thus pitches) attached by a common handle
double conical drum two-headed drum with a waist larger than the *drum head* on either end
double drumming a technique of playing the *snare drum* and *bass drum* simultaneously. The snare drum is tipped at a sharp angle and the bass drum is set vertically, making it possible to strike both drums with the sticks. It was used regularly before the development of the *bass drum pedal.*
double-stroke roll a method of sustaining sound on a drum by alternating two strokes from each stick in rapid succession. It is one of the standard drum *rudiments.*
douce (Fr.) soft
doumbek see *dümbelek*
doux (Fr.) soft
drag one of the standard snare drum *rudiments,* consisting of two grace notes, played as a double stroke, which embellish a single primary note
dragon's mouth see *temple blocks*
drahtbürste (Ger.) wire brushes
dreifacher vorschlag (Ger.) drag
Dresden timpani a model of pedal-tuned *timpani* with the tuning mechanism mounted on the outside of the bowl. A ratchet device secures the tuning pedal in position while the drum is fine tuned with a hand lever.
drinking glasses crystal beverage glasses which are struck or rubbed to sound a pitch. They may be tuned by adding or removing water from the container.
droite (Fr.) right
drome small *drum* or *tabor* used in medieval England

dromme Old English term for *drum*

drum a *membranophone* of varying size and shape found in virtually every culture. It consists of one or two heads stretched over a *drum shell,* which acts as a resonating cavity. It is sounded by striking with the hand, stick, or another implement.

drum cadence see *cadence*

drum chime in general, a drum which may be tuned to a musical pitch. Types of this instrument may be found in Africa and Asia.

drum gong a form of *tam-tam*

drum head the membrane, made of animal skin or plastic, which is stretched across a drum shell. On a *snare drum,* the top or struck head is the *batter head,* and the bottom is the *snare head.*

drum kit see *drum set*

drum machine an electronic instrument capable of producing sampled or synthesized sounds of *drums, cymbals,* or more commonly, an entire *drum set*

drum pad a device used as a practice instrument in place of a *drum*

drum roll a method of sustaining the tone on a drum. Different performing styles may use the *single stroke, double stroke,* or *closed roll.*

drum set a group of drums, cymbals, and auxiliary equipment, played by one drummer, used in jazz, rock, and popular music. Typical components include the *snare drum, bass drum, tom toms, hi-hat, ride cymbal, crash cymbal,* and the *bass drum pedal.*

drum stick implement used to play the *drums.* Sticks can be made of wood, plastic, metal, or other material.

drum stroke the movement of the player's arm, wrist, and fingers which sends the stick or mallet to strike the *drum*

drumslade (Ger.) obsolete term for a drummer

duck call a *bird call* used to imitate the quack of a duck

duff a generic term for a single-headed *frame drum,* occasionally with *jingles,* found in a number of cultures including Southern Europe, Northern Africa, Asia, and the Middle East

duggī hand drum from northern and central India, it is the lower pitched of a set of *tablā drums,* also known as the *banya.* It has a metal shell with a single skin head held on with leather straps. A circular patch of black paste is affixed to the center of the head to help focus the pitch of the drum.

dumbeg see *dümbelek*

dümbek see *dümbelek*

dümbelek single-headed *goblet drum* from Turkey. Similar to the *darabucca,* it is made from clay or copper, and used to accompany vocal music or the dance
dumpf (Ger.) muffled; muted
dur, dure (Fr.) hard
dura (It.) hard
duro (It., Sp.) hard

E

échelette (Fr.) obsolete term for the *xylophone*
effects see *sound effect instruments*
effektimstrumente (Ger.) sound effect instruments
effètto di piòggia (It.) rain machine
einfacher vorschlag (Ger.) flam
einfelltrommel (Ger.) single-headed drum
eisen (Ger.) iron
eisenschlägel (Ger.) iron beater
ejecutante (Sp.) performer; player
ekwe generic term for an African *slit drum*
Electra-vibe an electronically amplified *vibraphone,* manufactured by the J. C. Deagan Company in the 1970s
electronic percussion instruments electronic instruments which amplify or reproduce the sound of acoustic percussion instruments
elefantenglocken (Ger.) elephant bells
elephant bells small, brass *pellet bells* from India. They are made in various sizes and are shaken to activate the bell's internal clapper
en copa (Sp.) on the cup or *bell (of a cymbal)*
enclume (Fr.) anvil
end stroke combinations rudiments in Swiss *Basle drumming*
entenquak (Ger.) duck call
enveloppe en fil de laine (Fr.) covered in yarn or wool
eolifono (It.) wind machine
éoliphone (Fr.) wind machine
épaisse (Fr.) thick
éperons (Fr.) spurs
éponge (Fr.) sponge
escobilla (Sp.) wire brushes

esecutóre (It.) player
esquila (Sp.) cowbell
esquiletas (Sp.) xylophone
estaca (Sp.) stick
estremità (It.) at the end; at the rim
étouffé (Fr.) mute; dampen; *muffled*
étouffez (Fr.) muted; *muffled*
étouffez le son (Fr.) dampen the sound; *muffled*
exécutant (Fr.) player

F

faßtrommel (Ger.) barrel drum
faust (Ger.) fist
fell (Ger.) skin; drum head
feltro (It.) felt
fer (Fr.) iron
ferrinho (Braz.) triangle
fèrro (It.) metal
fèrro del triangolo (It.) metal *triangle* beater
fesselstabreibtrommel (Ger.) *friction drum* with fixed stick
feutre (Fr.) felt
fibra (Sp.) fiber
field drum a deep *snare drum,* often used in military or rudimental music
fieltro (Sp.) felt
fil (Fr.) thread; yarn
file a metal or wood rasp tool which is drawn against the edge of a *cymbal*
fill a short ad-lib section in *drum set* music, meant to be "filled" with a brief solo or rhythmic figure to set up an ensemble section
filo (Fr.) thread; yarn
filz (Ger.) felt
filzschlegel (Ger.) felt-headed stick
finger cymbals small *cymbals* played by striking the edges together. See also *zils.*
finger roll method of using friction to sustain sound on a *drum* or *tambourine* by rubbing a finger across the surface of the head. See also *thumb roll.*

fingerbecken (Ger.) finger cymbals
fingercymbeln (Ger.) finger cymbals
fingerzimbeln (Ger.) finger cymbals
fire bell a bronze cast *bell* struck by a hammer or metal striker. Used as a fire *alarm bell.*
fischiétto (It.) whistle
fischiétto a pallina (It.) pea whistle; police whistle
fischio (It.) whistle
fischio d'uccello (It.) bird whistle
fischio sirèna (It.) siren whistle
fissato (It.) fixed; attached
fixée (Fr.) fixed; attached
flagèllo (It.) whip; slapstick
flam one of the standard drum *rudiments,* it is a single grace note played before a primary note, the two struck with alternating hands
flamacue one of the standard drum *rudiments,* it is a combination of flams and accented single strokes
flaschenkorkenknall (Ger.) pop gun
flaschenspiel (Ger.) tuned bottles
flauta a culisse (Sp.) slide whistle
flauto a culisse (It.) slide whistle
flesh hoop the thin hoop of metal or wood which holds the *drum head.* The head is curled around the hoop and then placed on the *drum shell.* The *counter hoop* presses down on the flesh hoop, stretching it over the drum shell and putting tension on the head. *Calf skin heads* are tucked around the flesh hoop, while the modern plastic heads are crimped inside an aluminum hoop.
flessatono (It.) flexatone
flexaton (Ger.) flexatone
flexatone *sound effect instrument* consisting of a piece of spring steel with one end fixed in a handle frame. Small wooden balls attached to either side of the steel strike the plate when it is shaken. The pitch is changed by bending the steel as it is struck.
floor tom tom deep and low-pitched *tom tom,* single or double-headed, which stands on the floor at the extreme side of the *drum set*
fog horn *sound effect instrument* used to imitate a ship or lighthouse horn.
foglie di rame (It.) metal wind chimes
foglio di metallo (It.) foil rattle
foil rattle a sheet of thin, light metal which is shaken to produce a rattling sound. The largest example of this is the *thunder sheet.*

foot cymbal see *hi-hat*

fouet (Fr.) whip; slapstick

fouetter (Fr.) to strike; to whip

four-row xylophone an early form of the *xylophone* with the bars laid in a pattern four rows across

frame drum a single-headed drum with a narrow shell, usually struck with the hands or small beaters. Some instruments may have *jingles* (like a *tambourine*) or small bells attached to the frame.

frame rattle a rattle with *jingles,* discs, or other objects fixed or suspended inside a hand-held frame which strike against each other and the frame itself when the instrument is shaken

frappé, frappée (Fr.) struck

frappez (Fr.) to hit; to strike

fregare (It.) to rub; to strike

frei becken (Ger.) free cymbal; i.e., suspended cymbal

freihängend (Ger.) freely suspended; i.e., suspended cymbal

French cymbals thin to medium-thin weight *cymbals,* generally used when performing French orchestral literature

French flam see *flam*

French grip method of holding mallets or sticks, with the shaft held between the thumb and first finger, the palm vertical, and the thumb on the top of the stick

friction drum a drum sounded by friction on or against the head. Examples include the *cuíca, dog bark,* and *lion's roar.*

frigideira (Por.) small *frying pans,* struck with a stick, used in Brazilian music

frikyiwa (Af.-Akan) a small, metal, castanet-like bell with a high, sharp, clear tone. It is struck with a circular metal ring that is worn around the thumb.

frog drum see *bronze drum*

frôler (Fr.) to graze; to brush against

frottées (Fr.) to rub or strike together

frotter (Fr.) to rub; to strike

frullo (It.) friction drum

frusta (It.) whip; slapstick

frying pans metal cooking pans which give a gong-like sound when struck on the bottom

furitsuzumi small double-headed Japanese drum with wooden balls on strings which are tied to the shell. The balls strike the heads when the drum is rotated back and forth.

fußbecken (Ger.) hi-hat

fußmaschine (Ger.) bass drum pedal
fußschlegel (Ger.) bass drum pedal
fußstimmvorrichtung (Ger.) pedal timpani
fusta (Sp.) whip; slapstick
fusto (It.) frame; drum shell
fût (Fr.) drum shell; timpani bowl

G

gabelbecken (Ger.) cymbal tongs; metal castanets
gagaku drum double-headed Japanese drum
gambang a wood, bamboo, or metal *xylophone* used in Indonesian *gamelan* orchestras
gamelan percussion orchestra of Java, Bali, and Indonesia consisting of tuned *gongs, xylophones, metallophones, drums,* and occasionally string or wind instruments
gamelan gong a tuned metal *gong* with a raised center button or *boss,* used in *gamelan* ensembles
gangária Cuban or Latin American *cowbell*
gankogui (Af.-Ewe) an iron *double bell.* See also *agogo bells.*
ganugbagba (Af.-Ewe) literally a metal bucket played with two wooden *drum sticks* and used as a *bell*
ganzá (Por.) tubular *metal shaker* from Brazil
gariglione (It.) carillon bells
garn (Ger.) yarn; thread
garnschlegel (Ger.) yarn mallet
gauche (Fr.) left
gebetsglocke (Ger.) *bell* used in temple or prayer services
gedämpft (Ger.) muted; *muffled*
gefäßrassel (Ger.) rattle; maracas
gegenschlagblöcke (Ger.) concussion blocks
gegenschlagstäbschen (Ger.) concussion sticks; claves
geläute (Ger.) ringing or pealing of *church bells,* including *animal bells* or *cowbells*
gendang Indonesian and Malaysian double-headed drum
gender mallet-played metal *bar percussion instrument* used in the *gamelan* ensembles of Bali and Java
genou (Fr.) knee

geophone double-headed drum filled with pellets which, when rotated, imitates the sound of ocean waves, or a *surf effect*

German grip another name for the *matched grip*

Germanic cymbals heavy-weight *cymbals*, generally used with orchestral literature by Wagner and other 19th-century German composers

geschlagen (Ger.) struck

gestrichen (Ger.) stroked; rubbed

gewirbelt (Ger.) rolled; drum roll

gewöhnlich (Ger.) customary; ordinary; i.e., play the instrument in the normal manner

gewöhnlich schlagen (Ger.) strike in the ordinary manner

gewöhnlicher schlägel (Ger.) strike with the customary beater

ghuṅgrū small metal *pellet bells* of India and South Asia, worn on wrists or ankles to accompany dancers

gigelira (It.) obsolete term for the *xylophone*

ginòcchio (It.) knee

gitterrassel (Ger.) angklung

glas-windglocken (Ger.) glass wind chimes

gläserspiel (Ger.) tuned glasses

glasharfe (Ger.) glass harp

glasharmonika (Ger.) glass harmonica

glaspapier (Ger.) sandpaper; sandpaper blocks

glass harmonica an instrument consisting of glass bowls or cups mounted on a rotating spindle or table. It is played by rubbing moistened fingers on the glass rims as they turn. Also known as the *armonica.*

glass harp a set of *drinking glasses,* tuned by adding water. They are struck with a mallet or rubbed on the rim with moistened fingers.

glasspiel (Ger.) tuned glasses

glasstäbchen (Ger.) glass wind chimes

glasstäbe (Ger.) glass wind chimes

gleich abdämpfen (Ger.) muffle quickly

gleichgriff (Ger.) matched grip

gli uccelli (It.) bird whistle

glissando a musical scale on a tuned percussion instrument, either ascending or descending, played rapidly and usually without articulation of individual notes. On *timpani* it is created by moving the tuning pedal during or after striking the note; on *bar percussion instruments* it is created by sliding the mallet across the bars.

glissando avec le lever (Fr.) pedal *glissando* on timpani
glissando avec pédale (Fr.) pedal *glissando* on timpani
glissando colla pedale (It.) pedal *glissando* on timpani
glissando mit pedal (Ger.) pedal *glissando* on timpani
glöckchen (Ger.) tubular bells; chimes
glocke (Ger.) bell
glocken (Ger.) chimes
glockenartig (Ger.) like a bell; bell-like
glockenplatten (Ger.) bell plates
glockenspiel (Ger.) *keyboard percussion instrument* with steel or aluminum *bars.* In printed music, it may refer to a *bell lyra,* as used in German military music, or *orchestra bells,* as used in concert music.
glockenspiel à clavier (Fr.) keyboard glockenspiel
glockenspiel mit tasten (Ger.) keyboard glockenspiel
goblet drum single-headed drum with a shell in the shape of a goblet, a wide head, and narrow body, common to Arabia and the Middle East
goma (Sp.) gum; rubber
gómma (It.) gum; rubber
gomme (Fr.) gum; rubber
gong large round metal alloy disc of definite pitch. It may be flat, as used in concert music, or with a raised button or *boss* in the center, as found in the *gamelan* orchestras of Java and Bali (see *gamelan gong*). Compare with *tam-tam.*

The terms tam-tam and gong are used interchangeably by composers. If the part calls for either instrument (but not both), it probably refers to the large orchestral tam-tam. When the part calls for both instruments, the tam-tam is the larger instrument and the gong the smaller. Gongs may also be notated as having a definite pitch.

gong à mamelon (Fr.) button gong
gong chime a set of graduated *button gongs,* performed by one or more players, used in Indonesian *gamelan* orchestras
gong cinesi (It.) Chinese gong; button gong
gong drum a large single-headed *bass drum* with a narrow shell
gong giapponése (It.) Japanese gong; button gong
gong giavanése (It.) Javanese gong; button gong
gong, water see *water gong*
gongo (Sp.) gong

gongon (Af.-Dag.) a deep-voiced double-headed *cylindrical drum,* also called a brekete. The drum is wrapped in cloth and the two heads are connected by a series of cords which are squeezed to change the pitch of the head. A single twine or gut snare lays across each drum head and is struck with a curved wooden stick.
gongstrommel (Ger.) steel drum
gourd rattle a calabash gourd filled with seeds or small pellets
gourd scraper a hollow calabash gourd with notches or ridges carved in the body, scraped with a stick or beater
gourd water drum a half-section of a hollow gourd which floats upside down in a container of water. The gourd is struck with a wooden spoon or small stick. See also *water drum.*
gourd xylophone *xylophone* with *resonators* made from calabash gourds
gràcido di ànitra (It.) duck call
gran cassa (It.) bass drum
gran cassa a una pèlle (It.) single-headed bass drum; gong drum
gran cassa e piatti (It.) bass drum and crash cymbals
gran tamburo (It.) bass drum
gran tamburo vecchio (It.) deep snare drum; long drum
grand tambour (Fr.) deep snare drum; long drum
grande (Fr., It.) large; big
grande cloche (Fr.) large church bell or steeple bell
grave (Fr.) bass, or low in pitch
Greek cymbals small, tuned cymbals or *crotales*
grelots (Fr.) sleigh bells; pellet bells
grelots de vaches (Fr.) cowbell
griff (Ger.) handle of a drum stick
griffklapper (Ger.) slapstick
grosse caisse (Fr.) bass drum
grosse caisse à pédale avec cymbals décrochable (Fr.) bass drum played by a foot pedal with a detachable *cymbal striker*
grosse caisse à pied avec cymbals (Fr.) bass drum played by a foot pedal with a *cymbal striker*
grosse caisse à une secule peau (Fr.) single-headed bass drum; gong drum
grosse caisse associée avec les cymbales (Fr.) bass drum with attached cymbal
grosse caisse avec pedale (Fr.) bass drum played by a foot pedal
grosse, große (Ger.) large, big
grosse rührtrommel (Ger.) large tenor drum
grosse trommel (Ger.) bass drum

grosse trommel mit aufgeschnalltern becken (Ger.) bass drum with attached cymbal
grosse trommel und becken (Ger.) bass drum and crash cymbals
grosse trommelschlägel (Ger.) bass drum beater
grosse trommelstock (Ger.) bass drum beater
grosses klappholz (Ger.) large wooden *clappers*
grzechotka (Pol.) rattle
guáchara notched stick of Latin America, played as a *scraper*
guero see *güiro*
guimbarde (Fr.) jew's harp
güiro elongated hollow gourd or vessel with notches or ridges carved in the body, which is scraped with a stick or beater
guirro (It.) güiro
guitcharo Latin American *gourd scraper*
gummi (Ger.) rubber
gun shot see *pistol shot*
guyada (Sp.) jawbone of an ass
gyorsan (Hun.) dampen; muffle

H

halb zur mitte (Ger.) in the middle
halbmond (Ger.) Turkish crescent
hammer large wooden or rawhide mallet or carpenter's hammer used to strike wooden planks or boxes
hammer-wood British term for *xylophone*
hammerings see *stickings*
hammers an early term for the mallets and beaters used to play *bar percussion instruments*
hand bells small, pitched bells with internal clappers and attached handles, usually arranged in diatonic or chromatic scale sets, which are shaken to sound their note. A hand bell choir has several players shaking one or more bells in a pre-determined order to perform a piece of music.
hand cymbals a pair of cymbals held in each hand by straps and clashed together. See also *crash cymbals.*
hand drum a single or double-headed drum played by strokes of the hand on the head or shell. Examples include the *conga drum, jembe, tambourine,* and *frame drum.*

hand-screw timpani see *hand-tuned timpani*
hand-tuned timpani timpani with T-shaped tension rods that are turned individually to change the pitch of the drum
händen (Ger.) hands
handglocke (Ger.) hand bells
handglockenspiel (Ger.) hand bells
handle castanets a pair of *castanets* mounted on a flat piece of wood, sounded by shaking or striking them against a surface. This type of castanet is used most often in concert settings.
handratsche (Ger.) ratchet
handtrommel (Ger.) hand drum
hanfschlegel (Ger.) yarn mallet
hängebecken (Ger.) suspended cymbal
hängend (Ger.) suspended
hängende becken (Ger.) suspended cymbals
hanging board see *sēmantron*
harmonica see *glass harmonica*
harmonica de bois (Fr.) xylophone
harmonica de Franklin (Fr.) glass harmonica
harmonica de verre (Fr.) glass harmonica
harness bells small *pellet bells* attached to a strap, originally used on sleigh horses. See also *sleigh bells.*
harpaphone (Ger.) early term for a type of *metallophone,* a predecessor of the *vibraphone*
harpe de verre (Fr.) glass harmonica
hart (Ger.) hard
hartgummischlegel (Ger.) hard rubber stick
hat see *Turkish crescent*
haut (Fr.) high
hauteur réelle (Fr.) sounds at written pitch
heerpauke (Ger.) an obsolete term for the *kettledrum,* as used in early military music
herd bells metal *animal bells* with an internal clapper, originally hung around the neck of herd animals to identify their location and ownership. See also *cowbell.*
herd cowbells see *herd bells*
herdengeläute (Ger.) cowbell
herdenglocke (Ger.) herd bell; cowbell
herunterstimmen (Ger.) bring down; lower in pitch
hi-hat a pair of small *cymbals* mounted vertically and operated by a foot pedal mechanism. Depressing the pedal lowers the top

cymbal to clash against the bottom cymbal. It is most often used with a *drum set.*

hi-hat becken (Ger.) hi-hat cymbals
hierro (Sp.) iron
high-hat see *hi-hat*
hoch (Ger.) high
hochet (Fr.) a child's toy *rattle*
höhe (Ger.) height, in relation to pitch
hojalata de trueno (Sp.) thunder sheet
holz (Ger.) wood
holz geschlagen (Ger.) wooden *drum shell*
holz-tom-tom (Ger.) barrel drum
holz-und schlaginstrument (Ger.) xylophone
holz-und strohinstrument (Ger.) xylophone
holzblock (Ger.) wood block
holzblocktrommel (Ger.) wood block
holzfass (Ger.) barrel drum
holzfiedel (Ger.) obsolete term for the *xylophone*
holzhammer (Ger.) wooden beater
holzharmonika (Ger.) obsolete term for the *xylophone*
holzklapper (Ger.) slapstick; whip
holzplattentrommel (Ger.) wood-plate drum
holzraspel (Ger.) wooden scraper; reco-reco
holzschlägel (Ger.) wooden *drum stick*
holzschlitztrommel (Ger.) slit drum
holzstäbe (Ger.) claves
holzstabspiel (Ger.) xylophone
holztrommel (Ger.) wood drum; slit drum
holzwindglocken (Ger.) wind chimes
hoof beats see *horse hooves*
hoofs see *horse hooves*
hoop see *rim*
hoop-crack British term for *rim shot*
horse hooves coconut shells or wooden blocks, split in half and hollowed out. They are struck on a hard surface to imitate the sound of horse hoof beats.
hourglass drum drum with a shell in the shape of a hourglass; i.e., with a waist narrower than the ends
huehuetl single-headed *wood drum* from Mexico
hufgetrappel (Ger.) horse hooves

hültze glechter (Ger.) obsolete term for the *xylophone*
hupe (Ger.) auto horn
hyōshigi two blocks of hard wood that are struck together, used in Japanese and Chinese theater music

I

idiofono a raschiamento (It.) scraper; rasp
idiófono raspado (Sp.) scraper; rasp
idiophone an instrument that produces its sound by the vibration of its body, when it is struck, shaken, rubbed, or plucked. Examples include *cymbals, bar percussion instruments, castanets, scrapers,* and *mbiras.*
idiophone râpé (Fr.) scraper; rasp
in der ferne (Ger.) in the distance; offstage
in der mitte (Ger.) in the middle
incudine (It.) anvil
Indian bells small *pellet bells,* often attached to leather straps or clothing, worn or shaken by American Indian musicians and dancers
Indian drum drums used by American Indians, with a wood or clay shell and one or two skin heads held in place by leather straps. They are struck by single sticks or beaters as accompaniment to singing and/or dancing.
Indian jingles small metal discs, similar to tambourine *jingles,* mounted in a wooden frame and shaken or struck. Used to accompany American Indian music and dance.
Indian tablās see *tablā drums*
Indianischer trommel (Ger.) American *Indian drum*
Indische schellenband (Ger.) *Indian bells* attached to an ankle strap. Also known as *ankle bells.*
innendämpfer (Ger.) internal damper; tone control
instruments à percussion (Fr.) percussion instruments
iron chains lengths of linked iron chain which are shaken or rattled
iron pipes metal pipes or tubes of varying lengths which are struck by metal beaters. They may be played singly or arranged in a scale.

J

jackdaw a British type of *friction drum; lion's roar*

jaltaraṅg small bowls of varying sizes from India. They are tuned by filling them with water and are struck with thin bamboo sticks.

Janissary music music of Turkish military bands (ca. 1400-ca. 1850) which included percussion instruments such as the *triangle, crash cymbals, bass drum, snare drum, tambourine,* and *Turkish crescent.* Some characteristics of this music and the instruments were used in concert music by Haydn, Mozart, Beethoven, and others.

Janitscharenmusik (Ger.) Janissary music

Janizary music see *Janissary music*

jante (Fr.) rim

Japanese block temple block

Japanese metal bar instrument metal *bar percussion instrument* with *resonators,* used by Puccini and others to simulate a Japanese instrument

Japanese temple bell cup-shaped bell which rests on a cushion and is struck with small rubber-tipped beaters. Also known as *dobači.*

Japanese tree bell see *bell tree*

Japanese wood block see *temple blocks*

Japanese wood chimes see *bamboo wind chimes*

Javanese gong see *button gong*

Jaw's harp see *jew's harp*

jawbone of an ass an actual jawbone of a mule or donkey. When it is struck, the teeth rattle. The modern equivalent is a *vibraslap.*

jazz cymbal small thin *cymbal* used on early jazz *drum sets,* now commonly known as a *splash cymbal*

jazz drum *tom tom,* as used on a *drum set*

jazzbesen (Ger.) wire brushes

jazzo-flûte (Fr.) slide whistle

jeden ton gleich abdämpfen (Ger.) dampen each note immediately

jembe African *hand drum* with a single skin head and a hourglass body

jeu à tubes (Fr.) tubular bells; chimes

jeu chromatique de cencerros (Fr.) chromatically tuned *cowbells*

jeu de bouteilles (Fr.) tuned bottles

jeu de cloche (Fr.) tubular bells; chimes

jeu de clochettes (Fr.) orchestra bells
jeux de cencerros (Fr.) tuned almglocken
jeux de timbres (Fr.) orchestra bells

This is a keyboard glockenspiel written for by some French composers. Although this instrument still exists, most players perform this repertoire on the standard orchestra bells. The range of a jeux de timbres is greater than the orchestral bells, so players must transpose passages that go above high C one octave lower and passages that go below low G one octave higher.

jeux de timbres à clavier (Fr.) keyboard glockenspiel
jeux de timbres à marteaux (Fr.) keyboard glockenspiel
jew's harp an instrument with a flexible tongue fixed in a metal or bamboo frame. The instrument is held against the mouth while its tongue is plucked with a finger and the player's mouth and teeth act as resonators.
jingle bells sleigh bells; pellet bells
jingle stick 1) metal tambourine *jingles* set into a frame with a handle, played by shaking or striking them against another object. 2) a drum stick with tambourine *jingles* nailed to the shaft.
jingle-ring a thin metal or wood disc with metal tambourine *jingles* set into the frame
jingles small *pellet bells* or flat metal tambourine jingles played by shaking or striking
jingling Johnny a metal staff or stick adorned with *pellet bells* and *jingles,* sometimes topped with a crescent moon. Originally used in *Janissary music,* it is shaken and struck rhythmically against the ground. Also known as a *Turkish crescent.*
jonc (Fr.) cane; rattan
juego de botellas (Sp.) tuned bottles
juego de campanas (Sp.) tubular bells; chimes
juego de timbres (Sp.) glockenspiel; orchestra bells

K

kagan (Af.-Ewe) a long, slender, wooden *barrel drum.* It has a single head and is played by striking two long, thin sticks flat across the *drum head.*

kalimba African *lamellaphone* with metal or wood tongues fixed on a hollow wood box that acts as a *resonator.* The tongues are plucked by the thumbs or fingers with the pitch of the tongues determined by their length. The instrument is also known by other names such as *mbira* and *sansa.*

kamesa tubular *metal shaker*

kameso tubular *metal shaker*

kanon, kanone (Ger.) cannon shot

kapok a type of silky fiber

kastagnetten (Ger.) castanets

kastan'ety (Rus.) castanets

kastaniety (Pol.) castanets

kazoo metal or plastic cylinder with a thin membrane that vibrates and buzzes when the instrument is blown

kegeltrommel (Ger.) conical drum

kelchgläser (Ger.) cup-shaped glasses; water goblets

kessel (Ger.) kettle; timpani *bowl*

kesselpauke (Ger.) kettledrum; timpani

kesseltrommel (Ger.) kettledrum; timpani

ketten (Ger.) chains

kettenrassel (Ger.) rattling *chains*

kettledrum single-headed bowl-shaped drum. It is tuned by hand-tension screws or mechanical devices. See also *timpani.*

ketuk *button gong* used in Javanese *gamelan* ensemble

keyboard glockenspiel a set of metal *orchestra bell* bars activated by a piano-style keyboard mechanism. It sounds two octaves above written pitch.

keyboard mallet instrument generic term for *mallet percussion instruments* with notes arranged like a piano keyboard, played by *mallets.* It includes the *xylophone, marimba, vibraphone,* and *orchestra bells.*

keyboard orchestra bells see *keyboard glockenspiel*

keyboard percussion instrument generic term for *mallet percussion instruments* with bars arranged like a piano keyboard. It includes the *xylophone, marimba, vibraphone,* and *orchestra bells.*

keyboard xylophone a set of wood *xylophone* bars activated by a piano-style keyboard mechanism

keyed glockenspiel see *keyboard glockenspiel*

keyed xylophone see *keyboard xylophone*

khanjeri small *frame drum* or *tambourine* from India

khol two-headed *conical drum* from India, with unequal size skin heads

kick drum *bass drum* in a *drum set*
kidi (Af.-Ewe) a medium-sized, single-headed, wooden *barrel drum* played with two wooden sticks
kinderspielzeugtrommel (Ger.) child's toy drum
kirchenglocken (Ger.) church bells
kit drum kit; drum set
klanghölzer (Ger.) claves
klangstäbe (Ger.) claves
klapper (Ger.) rattle; clapper
klappholz (Ger.) wooden clapper; slapstick
kláves (Rus.) claves
klaviaturglockenspiel (Ger.) keyboard glockenspiel
klaviaturxylophon (Ger.) keyboard xylophone
klavierglockenspiel (Ger.) keyboard glockenspiel
klavierxylophon (Ger.) keyboard xylophone
klaxon hand-cranked *auto horn*
klaxon à manivelle (Fr.) hand-cranked *auto horn*; *klaxon*
klein (Ger.) small; little; used as a diminutive adjective
kleine (Ger.) small; little; used as a diminutive adjective
kleine pauke (Ger.) piccolo timpani
kleine trommel (Ger.) snare drum
kleine trommel-stocken (Ger.) snare drum sticks
kleine trommeln (Ger.) snare drums
klingen lassen (Ger.) let ring; allow to vibrate, do not dampen
klingt oktave höher (Ger.) sounding an octave higher
klingt wie notiert (Ger.) sounding as written
kloboto (Af.-Ewe) a deep-voiced, single-headed wooden drum played with sticks
klöppel (Ger.) bell *clapper*
klöpper (Ger.) drum sticks
knarre (Ger.) ratchet; rattle
knieschlag (Ger.) strike on the knee
knitting needle metal knitting needle used to strike *cymbals* and other metal instruments
knöchels (Ger.) knuckles
knochenklapper (Ger.) bones
knut (Rus.) slapstick
kokosnußschalen (Ger.) coconut shells
kolokól'chiki (Pol.) glockenspiel
konustrommel (Ger.) conical drum
konzerttrommel (Ger.) concert drum; snare drum
kopf (Ger.) head; drum head

Korean blocks temple blocks
Korean multiboard whip a series of small boards, connected in a row by string, which, when shaken, produces a short, rattling noise, similar to a *rachet* or *bin-sasara*
Korean squeeze drum see *changgo*
Korean temple blocks see *temple blocks*
Korean wood blocks see *temple blocks*
kork (Ger.) cork
kotly (Pol.) kettledrums; timpani
kreuzschlag (Ger.) 1) cross sticking; 2) stick shot
krotalen (Ger.) crotales; finger cymbals
krystallophon (Ger.) glass harmonica
ksilofón (Rus.) xylophone
kuba-pauken (Ger.) timbales
kuckuck instrument (Ger.) cuckoo bird call
kuckuckspfeife (Ger.) cuckoo bird call
kuckucksruf (Ger.) cuckoo bird call
kuhglocke (Ger.) cowbell
kuhglocke ohne Klöppel (Ger.) cowbell without clapper
kuhschelle (Ger.) cowbell
kulintang *button gong* of Indonesia; 2) the Indonesian ensemble which uses kulintang and other gongs and drums
kundu tall hourglass-shaped drum of New Guinea with a single skin head
kuppel (Ger.) the bell of a cymbal
kürbis (Ger.) calabash gourd
kürbisraspel (Ger.) gourd rasp; güiro
kürbisrassel (Ger.) gourd rattle
kurz (Ger.) choked; short; *muffled*
kurzwirbel (Ger.) short *drum roll*
kyeezee thick brass plate in the shape of a pagoda which, when struck, emits a long sustained tone

~ L

l. v. abbreviation for *laissez vibrer*
laine (Fr.) wool
laissez vibrer (Fr.) let vibrate; allow to ring, do not dampen
lame d'un canif (Fr.) knife blade

lame musicale (Fr.) musical saw

lamellaphone an instrument with thin lamellae, or tongues, of wood or metal which vibrate when plucked by the thumbs or fingers. The pitch of the tongue is determined by its length. Examples include the *mbira* and the *jew's harp.*

lamina metalica (Sp.) thunder sheet

lana (It.) wool

landsknechtstrommel (Ger.) military *field drum,* a type of *long drum*

lang (Ger.) long; length

lasciar vibrar (It.) let vibrate; allow to ring, do not dampen

lasciare le cordes del tamburo (It.) release (loosen) the snares

lastra del tuòno (It.) thunder sheet

lastra di latta (It.) foil rattle; thunder sheet

lastra di metallo (It.) foil rattle; thunder sheet

lastra di sasso (It.) stone discs; lithophone

Lateinamerikanische timbales (Ger.) timbales

lathe a narrow, thin strip of wood, used in building construction, which is struck against a leather pad or hard surface

latigazo (Sp.) whip; slapstick

látigo (Sp.) whip; slapstick

leder (Ger.) leather

lederschlegel (Ger.) leather beater

legnetti (It.) claves

legni di rumba (It.) claves

légno (It.) 1) wood; stick; i.e., wooden snare drum stick(s); 2) wood block

leight (berührt) (Ger.) lightly touching

leise (Ger.) soft; low

lero-lero (It.) rasp; scraper

let vibrate an instruction to let the instrument ring or sound past the duration of its notated value. Usually applied to *cymbals, triangles,* and other sustaining instruments.

libres cymbale (Fr.) suspended cymbal

liège (Fr.) cork

likembe a type of *lamellaphone* common to east, central, and south western Africa

lilletromme (Dan.) snare drum

linguaphone an instrument with plucked tongues of metal or wood. See also *lamellaphone.*

linkes fell (Ger.) left drum head; drum on the left side of a multi-drum set-up

links (Ger.) left; on the left side
Linn drum an electronic *drum machine,* developed by Roger Linn
lion's roar a large *friction drum* with a rope knotted underneath its single head which sticks out of the top of the drum head. A rosined rag is pulled along the rope which causes the head to vibrate, imitating the roar of a lion.
litávry (Rus.) timpani
lithophon (Ger.) lithophone
lithophone a *keyboard percussion instrument* with *bars* made from stone
litofono (It.) lithophone
lochsirene (Ger.) siren
lockern (Ger.) to slacken; to loosen
log drum a hollow wooden box or tree trunk with one or more tongues or slats cut into the shell. The tongues are struck by hands or mallets, with the pitch determined by the length of the tongue.
long drum a deep *field drum,* usually associated with military-style music. As used in concert music, it may or may not have *snares* and may also be identified as *landsknechtstrommel* or *tambourin.*
loo-jon see *lujon*
lotos flute see *slide whistle*
lotosflöte (Ger.) lotos flute; slide whistle
low-boy a shorter predecessor of the modern *hi-hat*
löwengebrüll (Ger.) lion's roar
lug the metal casing attached to the side of a *drum shell*
lujon a hollow box which acts as a *resonator* for metal tongues of varying lengths that are attached to the top. The pitch of the tongue is determined by its length.
lungo (It.) long
lyra see *bell lyra*
lyra glockenspiel see *bell lyra*

M

macchina da scrivere (It.) typewriter
macchina dal vento (It.) wind machine
macchina di tuòno (It.) thunder sheet

maceta (Sp.) mallet
machine à écrire (Fr.) typewriter
machine à tonnerre (Fr.) thunder sheet
machine à vent (Fr.) wind machine
machine timpani *timpani* with all tuning screws operated simultaneously by a mechanical system. This includes instruments tuned by rotating the drum, a hand crank, a chain device, or by a foot pedal.
madera (Sp.) wood
màglio (Sp.) hammer; large mallet
maillet (Fr.) mallet
maillet de cloche (Fr.) chime mallet
mailloche (Fr.) large mallet; bass drum mallet
mailloche de grosse caisse (Fr.) bass drum mallet
mailloche en bois (Fr.) wooden mallet
main (Fr.) hand
mallet the rubber, cork, cord, or yarn wrapped implement used to play *keyboard percussion instruments*
mallet percussion instruments generic term for tuned *percussion* instruments played with *mallets.* It includes the *xylophone, marimba, vibraphone, orchestra bells,* and others.
mallets a generic term for *keyboard percussion instruments* played with a mallet, including the *xylophone, marimba, vibraphone,* and *orchestra bells.*
mama-dada roll an onomatopoeic phrase used to teach the *double-stroke roll*
mamelon (Fr.) nipple gong; button gong
manche (Fr.) handle
manche en jonc (Fr.) cane handle; rattan handle
mandolin roll *keyboard mallet instrument* roll made by placing one *mallet* above and one below the *bar,* then striking the note in rapid alternating strokes
mànico (It.) handle
mano (It., Sp.) hand
manual cymbals see *crash cymbals*
máquina de escribir (Sp.) typewriter
máquina de trueno (Sp.) thunder sheet
máquina de viento (Sp.) wind machine
maraca de métal (Fr.) metal maraca; metal rattle
maraca di metallo (It.) metal maraca; metal rattle
maracas a pair of *shakers* with handles, common to Latin American music. They are made from plastic, metal, or gourds and contain seeds or pellets which rattle when shaken.

marákas (Rus.) maracas

marching bells see *bell lyra*

marching machine a wooden rectangular frame with small blocks of wood suspended across cords on the interior of the frame. Holding the instrument by the frame, the blocks are struck rhythmically against a hard surface to imitate the sound of marching troops.

màrgine (It.) edge; rim

marimba *mallet percussion instrument* with tuned bars of wood or synthetic material. Instrument construction and playing style differs between cultures from Africa to South America. The modern concert instrument can range from 2 $^1/_2$ to 5 octaves and sounds at written pitch.

marimba con tecomates a diatonic *Mexican marimba* with gourd *resonators*

marimba cuache the smaller instrument in the Mexican *marimba doble*

marimba de arco a type of Mexican *marimba con tecomates* with *resonators* but no legs, played while suspended around the marimbist's neck

marimba doble an ensemble of two chromatic *marimbas* from Mexico; the larger is the *marimba grande* and the smaller is the *marimba cuache* or *requinto*

marimba gongs *metallophone* consisting of a series of metal plates fitted with *resonators,* giving a sound similar to the *vibraphone*

marimba grande the larger instrument in the Mexican *marimba doble*

marimba piccolo see *marimba cuache*

marimba tenor see *marimba cuache*

marimba-xylophone *mallet percussion instrument* with an extended range to encompass the low notes of the *marimba* and the high notes of the *xylophone.* They were manufactured in the 1920s and 1930s to combine the sound characteristics and range of both instruments. Also known as *xylorimba.*

marimbafono (It.) marimba

marimbaphon (Ger.) marimba

marimbaphone (Fr.) marimba

marimbula a large bass *lamellaphone* of Latin America, similar to the African *mbira*

mark tree a series of small metal tubes, graduated in size and suspended from a horizontal bar. The tubes are brushed with the fingers or a mallet to produce a *glissando* effect.

marteau (Fr.) hammer
martelli sul incudini (It.) hammers on anvils
martèllo (It.) hammer
martillo (Sp.) hammer
marúga *metal shaker* or metal *maracas* used in Cuban music
mascèlla d'àsino (It.) jawbone of an ass
maschinenpauke (Ger.) machine timpani
matched grip method of holding *drum sticks* or *mallets* so that each hand has a similar position. The stick is held between thumb and first finger with the palm facing the ground.
matraca South American *ratchet*
maultrommel (Ger.) jew's harp
mazza (Sp.) large mallet; bass drum mallet
mazza doppia (Sp.) double-headed *beater*
mazzuolo doppio (Sp.) double-headed *beater*
mbila a type of *mbira* found in southern and south-eastern Africa
mbira African *lamellaphone* with metal or wood tongues affixed to a hollow wood box, which acts as a resonator. The tongues are plucked by the thumbs or fingers. The pitch of the tongues is determined by their length. The instrument is also known by many names including *kalimba* and *sansa.*
media, medio (It., Sp.) medium
mehrere (Ger.) several; many
mehter Turkish military band which uses instruments of *Janissary music*
membrana (It.) membrane; drum head
membrane drum head
membranophone an instrument that produces its sound by the vibration of a *membrane, skin head,* or *drum head* stretched across its body. Examples include the *snare drum, bass drum, frame drum, friction drum,* and *timpani.*
messerklinge (Ger.) knife blade
metà (It.) middle
metal block anvil or cowbell
metal castanets *finger cymbals* mounted on spring tongs which are squeezed to strike the cymbals together. Also known as *cymbal tongs.*
metal marimba early name for the *vibraphone*
metal pipe a length of thick iron pipe, struck with a *hammer* or hard *beater.* The length of the pipe determines the pitch.
metal plate a flat slab of iron or resonant metal, struck with a *hammer* or heavy *beater*

metal rasp metal *scraper* with notches or ridges on its body
metal rattle *rattle* or *shaker* with a metal body
metal scraper *scraper* or *rasp* with notches or ridges on its metal body
metal shaker metal tube filled with pellets or seeds, also known as *chocalho*
metal tube shaker see *metal shaker*
metallblock (Ger.) metal block; anvil
metallfolie (Ger.) foil rattle
metallgefässrassel (Ger.) metal rattle
metallkastagnetten (Ger.) metal castanets
metallo (It.) metal
metallofono (It.) metallophone
metallophon (Ger.) metallophone
metallophone an instrument consisting of a series of tuned metal *bars.* They may be arranged in a single or double row and tuned chromatically, diatonically, or in another scale system. Examples include *orchestra bells, vibraphone,* and *gender.*
metallplatte (Ger.) metal plate
metallschlegel (Ger.) metal beater
Mexican bean see *pod rattle*
Mexican marimba a type of Central and South American *marimba* with thin membranes that cover small holes in the bottom of the *resonators.* When the bar is struck, the membrane vibrates, creating a buzzing tone in addition to the tone of the bar. Examples of these instruments include the *marimba grande, marimba cuache, marimba de arco,* and *marimba con tecomates.*
mezzo (It.) half; middle
milieu (Fr.) medium; middle
militärtrommel (Ger.) military drum
military drum a deep *snare drum,* usually played with *snares* engaged, used in military or rudimental music
millwheel stroke snare drum *rudiment* used in Swiss *Basel drumming*
mirdangam see *mrdanga*
mirliton a device with a thin membrane that vibrates to create a buzzing or nasal sound, such as a *kazoo*
mit (Ger.) with
mit becken (Ger.) with cymbals
mit dämpfer (Ger.) muted; muffled
mit dem daumen (Ger.) with the thumb; thumb roll
mit dem fingern (Ger.) with the fingers
mit dem griff (Ger.) with handle of the stick or mallet
mit dem händen (Ger.) with the hands

mit den fingern (Ger.) with the fingers
mit den händen (Ger.) with the hands
mit holzschlägel (Ger.) with a wooden stick
mit saiten (Ger.) with snares on
mit schnarrsaiten (Ger.) with snares on
mit tellern (Ger.) with crash cymbals
mitte (Ger.) center; middle
mittel (Ger.) medium
mòdo ordinàrio (It.) in the ordinary manner; i.e., play the instrument in the typical way or using the traditional beater
moins (Fr.) less
mokubio Japanese wooden drum used in Buddhist temple services, similar in sound to a *temple block*
mòlle (It.) soft
molto (It.) much; very
molto duro (It.) very hard
molto mòlle (It.) very soft
monkey drum a small, two-headed rope-tensioned drum with two knotted strings tied to the shell. As the drum is rotated rapidly the ends of the string swing and strike each of the heads.
mòrbido (It.) soft
morceau de fil de fer (Fr.) piece of iron wire, or thin triangle beater
moteur (Fr.) motor
motor horn see *auto horn*
motor off on the *vibraphone,* to play with the motor turned off, giving a pure tone rather than a vibrato effect
motor on on the *vibraphone,* to play with the motor turned on to create a vibrato effect
mou (Fr.) soft
mounted castanets a pair of *castanets* mounted on a board and held apart by elastic or springs, so they may be struck together using the fingers or soft mallets
mounted finger cymbals a pair of *finger cymbals* mounted to face each other, either on a metal tong or a device similar to a *castanet machine*
mounted tom toms small *tom toms,* in varying sizes, attached to the bass *drum shell* in a *drum set*
mouth siren see *siren whistle*
moyen (Fr.) middle; medium
mrdanga an elongated, barrel-shaped drum from India. The two skin heads are tuned and tensioned by leather straps and played using hands and fingers.

mrdangam see *mrdanga*

muffled an instruction to play with the *snares* off. It may also imply covering the *drum head* with a cloth to dampen the head's vibrations and create a muted tone.

When this term is applied to the snare drum, the part should be played with the snares off. When used with other percussion instruments, such as bass drum, timpani, or tenor drum, it means to cover or mute the head with a piece of felt or cloth. The foreign terms that have a similar meaning are: (Ger.) gedämpft, abdämpfen, dämpfen, (It.) copèrto, and (Fr.) étouffé.

muffled stroke a stroke used on *hand drums* and *frame drums* requiring the fingers to remain on the head, muffling the sound

multiple bounce roll see *closed roll*

multiple percussion the performance of two or more percussion instruments by one person

muruba (Af.-Akan) a short, single-headed drum played with two wooden drum sticks. There are two types of muruba: a high-sounding drum heard as the female voice, and a lower-sounding drum which serves as the male voice.

muschel-windglocken (Ger.) *wind chimes* made of sea shells

música turca (Sp.) Janissary music

musical bow see *berimbau*

musical glasses crystal beverage glasses which are struck or rubbed to sound a pitch. The pitch is determined by size and thickness and can be fine-tuned by adding water inside the glass.

musical saw a carpenter's hand saw used to play melodies by bowing or striking the blade with a mallet

musique turque (Fr.) Janissary music

Musser grip a manner of holding three or more *mallets* to facilitate playing multiple notes on a *mallet percussion instrument*

Musser roll a type of *roll* to sustain tone on a *mallet percussion instrument*. The mallets (three or more) strike the bars alternately, similar to an arpeggio. Also known as the *ripple roll*.

muta (It.) change

muta in (It.) change to; used in *timpani* music to notate a change of pitch

N

nabimba a *marimba* manufactured by the J. C. Deagan Company in the early 20th century which featured thin membranes in the lower *resonators* to replicate the sound of a *Mexican marimba*
nacaire (Fr.) nakers
nácara (Sp.) nakers
nacchera (It.) nakers
nacchera cilindrica (It.) cylindrical wood blocks
nacchere (It.) castanets
nach (Ger.) change to; used in *timpani* music to notate a change of pitch
nachtigallenschlag (Ger.) nightingale bird call
nadimba marimba with a thin vibrating membrane in the *resonator,* to simulate the sound of a *Mexican marimba*
nagāṙā *kettledrum* from the Middle East, usually played in pairs in military and ceremonial music, but also used in folk and dance music
nakers small *kettledrums* with clay or metal shells and skin heads. Used in medieval Europe, they were a predecessor of the modern *timpani.*
nakovál'nya (Rus.) anvil
naqqārah small *kettledrums* of Central Asia and the Middle East, with clay, metal, or wood shells covered by a skin head
naruco (It.) wooden wind chimes
natural played in the normal manner
naturale (It.) played in the normal manner
naturfell (Ger.) skin head
nebelhorn (Ger.) fog horn
nietenbecken (Ger.) sizzle cymbal
nightingale bird call *whistle* with a water chamber and a blow pipe used to imitate the bird call
nipple gong see *button gong*
nòcce (It.) knuckles
noce di cocco (It.) coconut shells
noix de coco (It.) coconut shells
non vibrez (Fr.) no vibrato
normale (Fr.) customary, ordinary; i.e., play the instrument in the typical manner

ntrowa (Af.-Akan) a hollow *gourd rattle* without a surrounding net of beadwork

nur becken (Ger.) cymbals alone

oberreifen (Ger.) counter hoop

obertonkontrolle (Ger.) tone control; internal damper

ocean drum see *surf effect*

octamarimba see *octarimba*

octarimba *mallet percussion instrument* manufactured by the Leedy Drum Company in the 1930s. It featured adjacent wood *bars* tuned in octaves which are played by forked *mallets* with two heads.

octave marimba see *octarimba*

octobans a set of eight long, narrow diameter *tom toms,* each with a single head, played as tuned instruments in concert and *drum set* settings

ōdaiko general term for barrel-shaped drums with two tacked-on heads, used in Japanese kabuki theater music

oder (Ger.) or; otherwise

ohne (Ger.) without; excluding

ohne saiten (Ger.) without snares

ohne schellen (Ger.) without jingles

ohne schnarrsaiten (Ger.) without snares

okedo *cylindrical drum* with laced heads, used in the Japanese kabuki theater

on the rim direction to play on the *rim* or *counter hoop* of the instrument, usually on the *snare drum* or *bass drum*

on the wood see *on the rim*

ongle (Fr.) fingernail

open roll a method of sustaining tone on a drum by alternating two strokes from each stick. Also known as the *double-stroke roll,* it is one of the standard drum *rudiments.*

orchestra bells *mallet percussion instrument* with tuned steel *bars* played with brass, hard plastic, or hard rubber *mallets.* Used in concert music, the instrument has a minimum range of 2 1/2 octaves and sounds two octaves above the written pitch.

ordinaire (Fr.) customary, ordinary; i.e., play the instrument in the typical manner

ordinare (It.) customary, ordinary; i.e., play the instrument in the typical manner
ordinario (It.) customary, ordinary; i.e., play the instrument in the typical manner
ordinary an instruction to play the instrument in the typical fashion or with the standard *beater*
òrgano di légno (It.) xylophone
orilla (Sp.) edge; rim
orkesterglockenspiel (Ger.) orchestra bells
orlo (It.) edge; rim
ottóne (It.) brass

P

paar (Ger.) pair
paarweise becken (Ger.) pair of cymbals; crash cymbals
paddle castanets a pair of *castanets* mounted on either side of a flat piece of wood with a handle. When shaken or struck against a surface, the castanets clap against the wood and not against each other. They are used most often in concert music settings.
pailla (Sp.) timbale *drum shell*
pàio (It.) pair
pàio di piatti (It.) pair of cymbals; crash cymbals
paire (Fr.) pair
paire de cymbales (Fr.) pair of cymbals; crash cymbals
palillo baqueta (Sp.) wooden drum stick
palo (Sp.) stick
palo bufonesco (Sp.) slapstick
palo zumbador (Sp.) bull roarer
palochka (Rus.) drum stick
pan generic name for the steel pan or *steel drum*
pandeiro (Por.) large *tambourine* common to Portugal, Brazil, and Spain
pandereta (Sp.) tambourine
pandereta brasileño *jingle stick* used in Latin American and Brazilian music
pandéréta brésilienne (Fr.) pandereta brasileño; jingle stick
pandero (Sp.) tambourine
pandero sia sonajas (Sp.) tambourine without jingles; frame drum

pandéros Spanish *frame drums,* constructed in various sizes

pang cymbal see *Chinese cymbal*

panhuehuetl *cylindrical drum* of Central America used by the Aztecs

papel di lija (Sp.) sandpaper blocks

paper drum a small, two-headed Chinese drum mounted on a handle with two small balls tied to the shell. As the drum is rotated by turning the handle, the balls swing and strike the heads.

papier de verre (Fr.) sandpaper blocks

pappe rassel (Ger.) pasteboard rattle

par (Sp.) pair

parade drum a deep *snare drum,* played with *snares* engaged, used in military or rudimental music and on the march

paradetrommel (Ger.) parade drum

paradiddle one of the standard drum *rudiments,* it is a combination of single and double strokes in the pattern of RLRR or LRLL

parar (Sp.) to stop; dampen; mute

parche (Sp.) drum head

Parsifal bells a model of *orchestra bells* made in the1920s by the J. C. Deagan Company. They featured a rounded striking surface and a *resonator* under each bar.

Parsifal chimes four large bells, tuned to the pitches C, G, A, and E, used in Wagner's *Parsifal.* The tones may be played by specially constructed instruments using piano strings that are struck by mallets or by hand.

pas de cheval (Fr.) hoofbeat; horse hooves

pasteboard rattle small *friction drum* with a single skin head. A cord is knotted under the head and strung through the top of the head to loop around a small stick. As the drum is spun in the air, the head vibrates with a buzzing sound.

patouille obsolete term for *xylophone*

pattigame (Af.-Ewe) a small, high-pitched, double-headed metal shell drum. It is rested on the player's thigh and held by one hand which also presses fingers against the head to change the pitch and tone, while the other hand strikes the head with a wooden stick.

pauke (Ger.) timpano

pauken (Ger.) timpani

paukenfell (Ger.) timpani drum head

paukenschlägel (Ger.) timpani mallet

paukenwirbel (Ger.) timpani roll

pavilion see *Turkish crescent*
pavillon chinois (Fr.) Turkish crescent
pea whistle see *police whistle*
peau (Fr.) skin head; drum head
peau de batterie (Fr.) batter head
peau de tambour (Fr.) drum head
peau de timbre (Fr.) snare head
peau naturelle (Fr.) skin head
peau supérieure (Fr.) batter head
pedal cymbal 1) hi-hat; 2) a *cymbal* attached by a clamp to a bass drum *rim.* As the foot pedal strikes the *bass drum,* an attached metal *beater* simultaneously strikes the cymbal.
pedal drum see *pedal timpani*
pedal timpani *timpani* with a tuning mechanism operated by a foot pedal
pedalbecken (Ger.) hi-hat cymbals
pedale apèrto (It.) open hi-hat pedal (cymbals apart)
pedale chiuso (It.) closed hi-hat pedal (cymbals together)
pédale de la grosse caisse (Fr.) bass drum pedal
pedale della gran cassa (It.) bass drum pedal
pedalpauke (Ger.) pedal timpani
peitsche (Ger.) whip; slapstick
peitschenknall (Ger.) whip; slapstick
pèlle (It.) skin head; drum head
pèlle battende (It.) batter head
pèlle cordiera (It.) snare head
pèlle superiore (It.) batter head
pellet bell a small, hollow metal container with a ball or pellet inside that rattles and jingles when shook. They are used on *sleigh bells, ankle bells, jingling Johnny,* and other instruments.
pequeño (Sp.) small
percossa (It.) percussion
percuòtere (It.) to hit, beat, or shake
percusion (Sp.) percussion
percussão (Por.) percussion
percussion generic term for instruments that create their sound by striking, shaking, or vibrating
percussion sticks sticks that are struck against each other or against other instruments
percussione (It.) percussion
perdendosi (It.) dying away
perkusie (Pol.) percussion

perkussion (Dan., Swe.) percussion
Persian temple bells a series of cylindrical or conical metal bells, graduated in size and suspended by a string inside one another. They are sounded by striking or shaking.
petia (Af.-Akan) a short, single-headed, carved wooden drum struck with sticks
petit (Fr.) small; little
petit tambour (Fr.) small snare drum
petite (Fr.) small; little
petite caisse claire (Fr.) small snare drum; piccolo snare drum
petite tambour (Fr.) small drum; snare drum
petite timbale (Fr.) piccolo timpani
pī phāt instrumental ensemble from Thailand consisting of *bar percussion instruments,* tuned *gongs, drums,* and occasionally wind or string instruments
piano africano (Sp.) marimba
piatti (It.) cymbals
piatti a due (piatti a 2) (It.) crash cymbals
piatti a pedale (It.) hi-hat cymbals
piatti antichi (It.) antique cymbals
piatti attachi alla gran cassa (It.) bass drum with attached cymbal
piatti soli (It.) cymbals played alone, without bass drum
piatti sospesi (It.) suspended cymbal
piatto (It.) one cymbal; suspended cymbal
piatto cinesi (It.) Chinese cymbal
piatto fissato (It.) fixed cymbal; suspended cymbal
piatto sospeso (It.) suspended cymbal
piatto sospeso con bacchétta (It.) suspended cymbal struck with a stick
piatto sospesso al leggio (It.) bass drum with attached cymbal
piatto unito alla gran cassa (It.) bass drum with attached cymbal
piccolo (It.) small
piccolo cassa (It.) small *snare drum*
piccolo snare drum small, high-pitched *snare drum,* approximately 3 inches in depth
piccolo timpani small *timpani,* approximately 23 inches or smaller, with a pitch range in the upper bass clef
piccolo timpano orientalo (It.) a pair of small *timpani* with a range of notes in the lower and middle treble clef. See also *timplipito.*
pied (Fr.) foot; with foot pedal
piède (It.) foot; with foot pedal
pierres (Fr.) stones

piètra (It.) stones
pikkolotrommel (Ger.) piccolo snare drum
piòggia di effetto (It.) rain machine
pipe see *metal pipe*
pipe and tabor pair of instruments used in the 15th and 16th century to accompany dance music. The pipe resembles a small recorder and is played with one hand, while the *tabor* is a narrow shell, double-headed drum, suspended from the arm holding the pipe and struck by a stick held in the opposite hand.
pistol shot a blank round fired from a hand-held *revolver* to imitate the sound of a gun shot
pistolenschuß (Ger.) pistol shot
pistolettata (It.) pistol shot
plancha de campana (Sp.) bell plate
planchette ronflante (Fr.) bull roarer
plaque de métal (Fr.) metal plate
plaque de tonnerre (Fr.) thunder sheet
plastikfell (Ger.) plastic *drum head*
plates crash cymbals
platillo (Sp.) cymbal
platillo de dedo (Sp.) finger cymbals
platillo suspenso (Sp.) suspended cymbal
platillos a pares (Sp.) crash cymbals
plato charles (Sp.) hi-hat
platos (Sp.) cymbals
plattenglocke (Ger.) bell plate
pod rattle a dried pea or bean pod with seeds inside that rattle when the pod is shaken
podvéshennaya tarelka (Rus.) suspended cymbal
pogremúshka (Rus.) rattle
poing (Fr.) fist
police siren high-pitched *siren* as used on a police car
police whistle metal *whistle* with a pea or small pellet inside a hollow chamber. When blown, the pellet oscillates, creating a shrill tone.
politshkoi (Rus.) soft mallet
polizeiflöte (Ger.) police whistle
pollice (It.) thumb
pop gun *sound effect instrument* to imitate a cork popping from a champagne bottle, consisting of a tube, closed at one end by a cork, with a handle at the other end. As the handle is pumped, air pressure increases in the tube and forces the cork to pop out.

posée à plat (Fr.) laid flat
pouce (Fr.) thumb
prato de bronze (Braz.) *cymbal*
pratos (Por.) plates; crash cymbals
prayer bells see *dobači*
prayer stones small, smooth, flat stones which are struck or clicked together
pre-tuned drum head plastic *drum head,* tightened to playing tension, which is secured in a metal rim. The heads sound a tone when struck even without being tightened by tension lugs on a *drum shell.*
prendre (Fr.) change to; take
près de rebord (Fr.) near the edge; near the rim
press roll a method of sustaining tone on a drum by pressing the sticks into the *drum head* using rapid alternating strokes. It is similar to, but shorter duration than a *closed roll.*
preßwirbel (Ger.) press roll
prisme de pluie (Fr.) rain machine
pritsche (Ger.) slapstick
protubérance du milieu (Fr.) bell of a cymbal
provencal tambourin (Fr.) tabor
provenzalische trommel (Ger.) tambourin provençal
pugno (It.) fist
puita South American *friction drum*
pulgar (Sp.) thumb
pulgaretas small Spanish *castanets*
puño (Sp.) fist

Q

quail bird call *whistle* with a sliding plunger used to imitate the call of a quail
quasi cannone (It.) instruction to play in imitation of a *cannon shot*
queue (Fr.) tail; butt end of the *drum stick*
quica see *cuíca*
quijada (Sp.) jawbone of an ass
quinto the smallest size of *conga drum*
quyada (Fr.) jawbone of an ass

R

racle (Fr.) rasp; scraper
racleur (Fr.) to scrape; rasp
raganèlla (It.) ratchet
rahmenrassel (Ger.) frame rattle
rahmentrommel (Ger.) frame drum
rail d'acier (Fr.) steel rail or steel bar
rain machine *sound effect instrument* to imitate the sound of rain. In concert music, it is a large drum with a wire mesh shell set in a wood frame. The drum is filled with small balls or pebbles and rotated by a crank, causing the balls to tumble around inside the shell. A smaller instrument is known as a *rain stick.*
rain stick *sound effect instrument* to imitate the sound of rain. A tube of bamboo, cactus, or plastic is filled with seeds or pellets which slide down the length of the tube as the instrument is turned upside down.
rānat a family of *xylophones* and *metallophones* from Thailand and Southeastern Asia, which includes the rānat ek, rānat thum, ranēt ēk lek, and ranēt thum let
rand (Ger.) rim; edge
rand und fell zugleich schlagen (Ger.) strike the rim and the head at the same time; *rim shot*
randschlag (Ger.) rim shot
râpe (Fr.) rasp
râpe à fromage (Fr.) cheese grater; metal rasp
râpe de bois (Fr.) wooden rasp
râpe de métal (Fr.) metal rasp
râpe guiro (Fr.) güiro
râper (Fr.) to rasp
râpeur (Fr.) rasp; scraper
rasch abdämpfen (Ger.) dampen quickly
rasp a block or stick made of gourd, wood, or metal, with serrations on the body. It is scraped with a small stick, similar to the *güiro.*
raspa (It., Sp.) rasp; scraper
raspa di metallo (It.) metal rasp; metal scraper
raspadero (Sp.) rasp; scraper
raspador (Sp.) rasp; scraper

raspador metal (Sp.) metal rasp; metal scraper
raspar (Sp.) to rasp; to scrape
raspare (It.) to rasp; to scrape
raspel (Ger.) rasp; scraper
rasper see *rasp*
rasping stick wooden stick with serrations cut in the body, scraped like a *rasp*
raspo (It.) rasp; scraper
rassel (Ger.) rattle
rasseltrommel (Ger.) rattle drum
ratamacue one of the standard drum *rudiments,* it is a pair of double-stroked grace notes which ornament a triplet figure
ratchet a wooden wheel with cogs or serrations which is turned by a crank or spun on a handle, causing wooden slats to slap against the cogs
ratsche (Ger.) ratchet
rattle an instrument that creates noise when shaken or beaten. It may be a hollow container with loose items inside, such as *maracas,* or a device with parts that clatter against each other, such as a *sistrum.*
rattle drum a small, two-headed *drum* with two small balls tied by strings to the shell. As the drum is rotated or spun rapidly, the balls swing and strike the heads.
rebord (Fr.) edge; rim
rechtes fell (Ger.) right *drum head*; drum on the right-hand side
rechts (Ger.) right; on the right hand side
reclamo (Sp.) bird call
reco-reco (Por.) a hollow *bamboo scraper,* similar to the *güiro,* common to Brazilian music
redoblante (Sp.) tenor drum
redoble (Sp.) drum roll
regenmaschine (Ger.) rain machine
regenprisma (Ger.) rain machine
reggipiatto (It.) cymbal stand
reggitamburo (It.) drum stand
regimental drum *field drum,* which usually plays with trumpets in trio strains of military marches
reibtrommel (Ger.) friction drum
reifen (Ger.) counter hoop; rim
reihenklapper (Ger.) bin-sasara
repinique (Por.) metal *tom tom,* the tenor voice in the Brazilian samba school percussion ensemble

reprenez (Fr.) repeat; continue
reque-reque scraped instrument, similar to the *reco-reco*
requinto the smaller instrument in the Mexican *marimba doble*
reso-reso (It.) reco-reco
resonanzkastenxylophone (Ger.) trough xylophone
resonanzrohr (Ger.) vibraphone resonators
résonateur (Fr.) resonators
resonator in general, a body such as a hollow shell, gourd, or tube which helps enhance the tone of an instrument
resonatoren (Ger.) resonators
resonators hollow tubes made of metal, cardboard, wood, or gourds which are placed under the *bars* of *mallet percussion instruments* to enhance the tone and the tuning. The tube is closed at one end at a length which corresponds to the pitch of the bar.
revolver a hand-held pistol which fires blank rounds to imitate the sound of a gun shot
rhombe (Fr.) bull roarer
rhythmusstöcke (Ger.) rhythm sticks; percussion sticks
ribeba (It.) jew's harp
richiamo de uccelli (It.) bird call
ricopèrta (It.) covered [with]
ricopèrta in pelle (It.) leather-covered [mallet]
ricopèrto (It.) covered [with]
ride cymbal a *suspended cymbal* on a *drum set,* approximately 16 to 24 inches in diameter, used to play repeated rhythmic patterns
rim a hoop of metal or wood that presses down on the *flesh hoop* and puts tension on the *drum head* by stretching it over the edge of the *drum shell.* Tension rods or clamps attach to the rim to tighten the head. It is also known as the *counter hoop.*
rim shot drum stroke that strikes the *rim* and the *drum head* simultaneously. Compare with *stick shot.*
ringing stones see *lithophone*
ripple roll see *Musser roll*
riqq Arabian *frame drum*
rivet cymbal see *sizzle cymbal*
rivoltèlla (It.) revolver
rivoltellata (It.) revolver shot; pistol shot
rnga large and narrow double-headed drum of Tibet, used in Buddhist ceremonies
rock gong see *lithophone*
rock harmonica see *lithophone*
rohr (Ger.) rattan; bamboo

röhrenglocken (Ger.) tubular bells; chimes
röhrenglockenspiel (Ger.) tubular bells; chimes
röhrenholztrommel (Ger.) cylindrical wood block
röhrenrassel (Ger.) tubular rattle
röhrentrommel (Ger.) barrel drum
rohrschlegel (Ger.) rattan or cane stick
rohrstäbschen (Ger.) rattan sticks
roll a method of sustaining tone on a percussion instrument by rapidly alternating sticks or mallets
roll off rhythmic pattern, usually eight beats in length, played by a marching percussion section as a signal for the band to begin playing a musical selection
rolliertrommel (Ger.) tenor drum
rollo (It.) drum roll
rollschellen (Ger.) pellet bells; sleigh bells
rolltrommel (Ger.) tenor drum
rómbo sonore (It.) bull roarer; friction drum
rommelpot European *friction drum* from the 1600s. The body is a small clay pot with a skin stretched across the opening and a small stick protruding from the head.
roncador Latin American *friction drum*
rope drum *military drum* with the heads tensioned by a rope strung alternately through the top and bottom hoops around the circumference of the shell. The heads are tightened or loosened by sliding leather tabs along adjacent strands of the rope.
rosewood a hard wood native to Honduras in Central America, preferred as a material to construct *bars* for *mallet percussion instruments*
rotary-tuned timpani *timpani* with tuning rods that tighten and loosen the head which operate simultaneously by turning the *bowl* which sits on a master screw
rotin (Fr.) rattan; i.e., rattan mallets
roto tom accordé manuellement (Fr.) hand-tuned roto tom
roto tom afinado a mano (Sp.) hand-tuned roto tom
roto tom hangestimmt (Ger.) hand-tuned roto tom
roto toms single-headed tunable *tom toms* without a *drum shell*. The pitch is changed by rotating the drum's *rim* which sits on a central master screw that tightens and loosens the *drum head*.
roulante (Fr.) rolling
roulement (Fr.) drum roll
rouler (Fr.) to roll

roulez (Fr.) drum roll
row rattles a group of small items, such as sea shells, animal teeth, and fruit husks, which are strung together and shaken or struck to create a rattling sound
rudimental drumming a style of drumming which is based on use of the standard drum *rudiments,* most commonly used in military or marching music
rudiments fundamental strokes and patterns that are basic to all drum music and technique. There are over forty such patterns used in the rudimental style of snare drumming.
ruff one of the common drum *rudiments,* it is an ornament of 2 or more grace notes that embellish a primary note. See also *drag.*
ruggito di leóne (It.) lion's roar
rugir de león (Sp.) lion's roar
rugissement de lion (Fr.) lion's roar
rührtrommel (Ger.) tenor drum
rührtrommel mit saiten (Ger.) field drum; parade drum
rullare (It.) to roll
rullio (It.) drum roll
rullo (It.) drum roll
rumbabirne (Ger.) maracas
rumbahölzer (Ger.) claves
rumbakugeln (Ger.) maracas
rumbastäbe (Ger.) claves
rute (Ger.) a bundle of wooden rods or twigs. See also *switch.*
ruthe see *rute*

S

sablier (Fr.) sandbox
säge (Ger.) musical saw
saiten (Ger.) snares
saitenfell (Ger.) snare head
saitenschraube (Ger.) snare strainer
sake barrel small wooden barrel struck on its lid with wood sticks
sakefaß (Ger.) sake barrel
samba African *frame drum*
samba whistle metal *whistle* with three tone holes capable of three different pitches, used in Latin American dance music

sanctus bells three or four metal *hand bells,* attached to metal crossbars, which are shaken vigorously
sand blocks see *sandpaper blocks*
sand rattle small tin or metal containers filled with sand
sandblöcke (Ger.) sandpaper blocks
sandbox small tin or metal containers filled with fine grain sand or shot
sandbüchse (Ger.) sandbox
sandpaper blocks a pair of small wooden blocks, covered with sandpaper, which are rubbed against each other
sandpapier blöcke (Ger.) sandpaper blocks
sandrassel (Ger.) sand rattle; sandbox
sanduhrtrommel (Ger.) hourglass drum
sans (Fr.) without
sans cordes (Fr.) without snares
sans sourdine (Fr.) without mute
sans timbres (Fr.) without snares
sans tintements (Fr.) without jingles
sansa term often used as a generic name for an African *lamellaphone.* Thin metal or wood tongues are fixed on a hollow wood box, which acts as a resonator. The tongues are plucked by the thumbs or fingers, their pitch determined by their length. The instrument is also known by many other names such as *mbira* and *kalimba.*
sanza see *sansa*
sapo Cubana (It.) small *bamboo scraper*
sarna bell small *pellet bell* from India
saron *metallophone* used in the Javanese *gamelan* orchestra. Three sizes and ranges are used: saron demung (lowest), saron baruyng (middle range), and saron panerus or saron peking (highest).
sarténes *frying pans* mounted upside down and struck on the bottom to sound a gong-like tone. Used in Latin American folk music.
sassi (It.) stones; rocks
sbàttere (It.) to beat; to shake
scacciapensièri (It.) jew's harp
scampanellio da gregge (It.) cowbell
schallbecken (Ger.) cymbals
schallenglöckchen (Ger.) small bowl-shaped bells used in Buddhist temple ceremonies
schallstücke (Ger.) bell

schellbecken (Ger.) cymbals
schelle (Ger.) pellet bell
schellen (Ger.) sleigh bells; pellet bells
schellenbaum (Ger.) Turkish crescent
schellenbündel (Ger.) a group of *sleigh bells* or *pellet bells* bundled or mounted together
schellengeläute (Ger.) sleigh bells
schellenrassel (Ger.) jingles; jingle stick
schellenreif (Ger.) jingle-ring; *tambourine* without a head
schellenstock (Ger.) jingle stick
schellentrommel (Ger.) tambourine
schiffsglocke (Ger.) ship's bell
schirrholz (Ger.) bull roarer
schlag (Ger.) drum stroke
schlag mit Praller (Ger.) closed roll
schlagbecken (Ger.) crash cymbals
schlagbrett (Ger.) wooden board
schlägel (Ger.) drum stick
schlagen (Ger.) to hit; to strike; to beat
schlagfell (Ger.) batter head
schlaginstrument (Ger.) percussion instrument
schlaginstrumentengruppe (Ger.) percussion section; battery
schlagrassel (Ger.) jawbone of an ass; vibraslap
schlagstäbe (Ger.) percussion sticks; claves
schlagwerk (Ger.) percussion
schlagzeug (Ger.) percussion instruments; drum set
schlagzeuger (Ger.) drummer; percussionist
schlagzeugspieler (Ger.) drummer; percussionist
schlegel (Ger.) drum stick; mallet; beater
schlegelinstrumente (Ger.) mallet percussion instruments
schlittelrohr (Ger.) metal tube shaker
schlitten-schellen (Ger.) sleigh bells
schlittenglocken (Ger.) sleigh bells
schlitztrommel (Ger.) slit drum
schmirgelblock (Ger.) sandpaper block
schnarre (Ger.) rattle
schnarren (Ger.) to rattle
schnarrsaiten (Ger.) snares
schnarrtrommel (Ger.) snare drum
schnur-reibtrommel (Ger.) friction drum with cord; string drum
schotenrassel (Ger.) pod rattle
schraper (Ger.) scraper; rasp

schraubenpauke (Ger.) hand-tuned timpani
schraubenschlüssel (Ger.) [timpani] tuning handle
schreibmaschine (Ger.) typewriter
schütteln (Ger.) to shake
schüttelrohr (Ger.) shaker; chocalho
schwamm (Ger.) sponge; i.e., sponge beaters
schwammschlägel (Ger.) sponge-headed stick
schwirrholz (Ger.) bull roarer
scie musicale (Fr.) musical saw
scopèrto (It.) uncovered; not muffled; snares on
scopettine (It.) wire brushes
Scotch bass drum thin *bass drum,* played with hard felt mallets, used in Scottish *rudimental drumming* units
scraper a stick or hollow body made of gourd, wood, or metal, with serrations on the body. It is scraped with a small stick. Examples include the *güiro, rasp,* and *washboard.*
scratcher see *scraper*
scuòtere (It.) to shake
sec (Fr) dry; short duration
secco (It.) dry; short duration
secouer (Fr.) to shake
séga (It.) musical saw
sega cantate (It.) musical saw
sehr (Ger.) very
sekere see *shekere*
semanterion see *sēmantron*
sēmantron oblong wooden board, suspended and struck with a wooden *mallet* or *hammer,* used in the rites of the Greek Orthodox church
sèmpre (It.) always; ever
sènza (It.) without
sènza còrda (It.) without snares
sènza sordino (It.) uncovered; not muffled
serrucho (Sp.) musical saw
seule (Fr.) alone; solo
sguilla (It.) cowbell
shake roll method of sustaining sound on a *tambourine* by shaking the instrument to make the *jingles* rattle
shaker a hollow vessel, filled with pellets or seeds, which is shaken back and forth. Examples include the *chocalho* and *maracas.*
shaman drum single-headed *frame drum,* used in ritual acts and

ceremonies by shaman or religious leaders in Asia, India, and American Indian tribes

shekere large calabash gourd covered with a netting of beads, originally from Nigeria. The instrument is shaken to make the beads strike against the gourd.

shell chimes *wind chimes* made of sea shells

shellentrommel (Ger.) tambourine

shimedaiko generic term for narrow-bodied *barrel drums* used in Japanese theater music

ship's bell cast bronze *bell* with an internal clapper, used on navy ships or as an *alarm bell* or storm warning

ship's whistle sound effect to imitate a ship or lighthouse horn. It consists of several short pipes of metal or wood, blown through a common mouthpiece.

shoko *gong* used in Japanese gagaku court music

shränken (Ger.) to tension; to tighten

side drum British term for *snare drum*

sifflement (Fr.) whistling; hissing

sifflet (Fr.) whistle

sifflet à coulisse (Fr.) slide whistle

sifflet à roulette (Fr.) pea whistle; police whistle

sifflet coucou (Fr.) cuckoo bird call

sifflet d'oiseau (Fr.) bird whistle

sifflet imité du rossignol (Fr.) nightingale bird call

sifflet signal (Fr.) signal whistle

sifflet sirène (Fr.) siren whistle

signal whistle air-driven *whistles* used to signal warnings or alarms. Examples include the *police whistle, fog horn,* and *siren.*

signalpfeife (Ger.) signal whistle

silbato (Sp.) whistle

silbato del ave(Sp.) bird whistle

silbato sirena (Sp.) siren whistle

silofono (It.) xylophone

silofono a tastiera (It.) keyboard xylophone

silofono basso (It.) bass xylophone

silomarimba (It.) xylorimba

silophono (It.) xylophone

simandron see *sēmantron*

sin cuerdas (Sp.) without snares

sineta small *bell* used in South American music

singende säge (Ger.) musical saw

single stroke roll a method of sustaining tone on a percussion instrument by rapidly alternating one stroke from each stick. It is one of the standard drum *rudiments.*

sinistra (It.) left

sino *bell* used in South American music

siren air-driven *sound effect instrument* which creates a piercing tone that fluctuates in pitch, rising and falling in a *glissando.* Air is driven over a perforated disc which is rotated by a hand crank, electric motor, or breath blown through a *whistle.*

siren whistle small metal *whistle,* blown to produce the *glissando* sound of a *siren*

sirena (It., Sp.) siren

sirena a fiato (It.) siren whistle

sirena bassa (It.) fog horn

sirena da battèlo (It.) boat whistle; fog horn

sirene (Ger.) siren

sirène (Fr.) siren

sirène à bouche (Fr.) siren whistle

sirène aigue (Fr.) high-pitched *siren*; police siren

sirène grave (Fr.) low-pitched *siren*

sirenenpfeife (Ger.) siren whistle

sistra (It., Sp.) sistrum

sistre (Fr.) sistrum

sistro a set of small, bronze, cup-shaped bells mounted on a frame with a handle. They are a predecessor of the *keyboard glockenspiel. Orchestra bells* or *crotales* may be used as a substitute.

sistrum noisemaker consisting of a u-shaped frame set in a handle with small metal rods or wires spanning the opening. Metal discs are suspended on the rods and rattle when the instrument is shaken or struck.

The sistrum may also be a metal maraca. Lou Harrison writes for the sistrum in his percussion music and uses a metal maraca for this sound.

sizzle cymbal *suspended cymbal* with a metal device attached which creates a buzz or sizzle when the instrument is struck. The cymbal may have rivets inserted in it, a small chain or keys touching it, or a commercial sizzle unit attached.

skin head a *drum head* made of animal skin

skins slang term for *drum heads* or drums in general

slagwerk (Dut.) percussion

slapstick two wooden slats, hinged together at the base, which are struck together to create a loud slapping noise, used to imitate a *whip*

sleigh bells small *pellet bells,* either affixed to a strap as used on sled horses, or attached to a handle as used in concert music

slide whistle a metal, plastic, or wooden cylindrical tube with a movable plunger inside. The *whistle* is blown on one end as the plunger is slid the length of the tube to create a *glissando* effect.

slit drum a hollow wooden box or tree trunk with one or more tongues or slats cut into the shell. The tongues are struck by hands or mallets, with the pitch determined by the length of the tongue.

slung mugs ceramic cups or vessels of various sizes, suspended from a frame and struck with wood beaters

small drum British term for *snare drum*

smorzare (It.) to dampen

snare drum double-headed *drum* used for concert and *drum set* music. It is struck on the top head (*batter head*) which causes the vibration of the bottom head (*snare head*) and consequently the *snares* that rest against it.

snare head the bottom head of a *snare drum.* The *snares* rest against this head and vibrate in sympathy when the top or *batter head* is struck.

snare strainer the device, affixed to the *drum shell,* which raises and lowers the *snares* to touch the bottom head of a *snare drum*

snares gut, wire, cable, or plastic cords which are strung across the bottom head of a drum, known as the *snare head.* The snares vibrate in response to strokes on the *batter head,* and give the instrument a buzzing tone.

sock cymbals slang term for a *hi-hat*

sòffice (It.) soft

soffocare (It.) to choke; to muffle

soffocato (It.) choked; *muffled*

soli (It.) a solo part played by more than one player

sonagli (It.) sleigh bells; pellet bells

sonagli a mano (It.) hand bells

sonaglieri (It.) sleigh bells

sonaglio (It.) small bell; pellet bell

sonaja (Sp.) Central and South American *gourd rattle*

sonajero (Sp.) Mexican rattle

sonatóre (It.) player; musician

soneria di campane (It.) chimes

song bells *mallet percussion instrument* manufactured by the J. C. Deagan Company. The metal *bars* have *resonators* mounted underneath to enhance the tone quality. The sound resembles a *celesta* or *orchestra bells.*

song whistle see *slide whistle*

sonnaille (Fr.) cowbell

sonnailles de troupeau (Fr.) herd bells; cowbells

sonnette (Fr.) hand bell; pellet bell

sonnette de table (Fr.) dinner bell

sons réels (Fr.) sounds at written pitch

sons voilé (Fr.) muted; muffled

soprano metallophone *bar percussion instrument* developed for use with Carl Orff's schulwerk music education program. This metal bar instrument has a diatonic or chromatic written range from middle c to f on top of the treble clef staff and sounds one octave higher than written.

soprano xylophone *bar percussion instrument* developed for use with Carl Orff's schulwerk music education program. This wooden bar instrument has a diatonic or chromatic written range from middle c to f at the top the treble clef staff, and sounds one octave higher than written.

sordina (It., Sp.) mute; muffler

sordino (It.) mute; muffler

sordino interno (It.) internal muffler

sospenso (It.) suspended

sospesi (It.) suspended

sospéso (It.) suspended

sound effect instruments instruments played to imitate the sounds of animals or objects. Many were developed for use in vaudeville and as accompaniment to silent films. Examples include *lion's roar, dog bark, car horn, boat whistle, wind machine,* and many others.

sourd (Fr.) muted; muffled

sourdine (Fr.) mute; muffler

sourdine interne (Fr.) internal muffler; tone control

spannreifen (Ger.) counter hoop

spègnere (It.) to dampen; mute

speróni (It.) spurs

spieler (Ger.) player

spielsäge (Ger.) musical saw

splash cymbal thin *cymbal,* 6 or 8 inches in diameter, with a rapid response and a fast decay. As part of a *drum set,* it is used for special effects and accents.

sponge beaters early notation for soft *mallets,* now played with soft felt mallets on timpani and yarn, cord, or wound mallets on *suspended cymbals*

spoons wood or metal *clappers* in the shape of concave spoons. They are held between the fingers and are struck together, against the body, or across the spread fingers of the opposite hand.

sporen (Ger.) spurs

spring coil see *coil spring*

spring güiro three springs with adjustable tension mounted on a metal pipe with an oval opening. The springs are scraped and the opening is covered and uncovered to change the tone of the instrument.

sproni (It.) spurs

spugna (It.) sponge

spurs *sound effect instrument* consisting of metal discs strung on a metal rod set in a handle. The instrument is shaken or struck to imitate the jingle of spurs on cowboy boots.

stabglockenspiel (Ger.) orchestra bells

stabpandereta (Ger.) jingle stick

stahl (Ger.) steel

stahlspiel (Ger.) orchestra bells; glockenspiel

stahlstäbe (Ger.) 1) metal plate; 2) glockenspiel; orchestra bells

stahltrommel (Ger.) steel drum

stampfrohr (Ger.) stamping tube

stampftrommel (Ger.) stamping tube

stamping tube wood or bamboo tube which is struck rhythmically on the ground

stappare la bottiglia (It.) pop gun

starter's pistol hand-held *revolver* which fires blank rounds, used to imitate the sound of a *pistol shot*

steamboat whistle low-pitched *whistle,* made of wood or metal, used to imitate the horn of a river steamboat

steel band an ensemble of *steel drums*

steel bells see *orchestra bells*

steel discs see *steel plates*

steel drum tuned percussion instrument made from empty oil or gasoline drums. Areas on the top of the drum are marked and tuned to definite pitches. The pitch is determined by the size of the marked area and the depth of the drum body.

steel marimba steel bar *mallet percussion instrument* manufactured by the J. C. Deagan Company. It was a predecessor of the *vibraphone.*

steel pan see *steel drum*

steel plates thick discs or slabs of steel which are suspended by cords or on padded supports and struck with metal beaters. The size of the plate determines the pitch.

steeple bell see *church bell*

stein (Ger.) stone

steinplatten (Ger.) lithophone

steinspiel (Ger.) lithophone

stempelflöte (Ger.) slide whistle

Stevens grip a manner of holding four mallets to facilitate playing multiple notes on mallet percussion instruments

sticcada (It.) xylophone

sticcato (It.) xylophone

stick shortened form of the term *drum stick*

stick clicks rhythmic beat made by tapping one stick against the other, used for visual or special effects

stick on stick see *stick shot*

stick shot accented *drum stroke* made by placing the tip of one stick in the center of the *drum head* and striking its shaft with the other stick

stickings the pattern of left and right hand *drum strokes* used to facilitate stick patterns or play traditional *rudimental drumming* figures

stiel (Ger.) handle

stock (Ger.) drum stick

stock auf stock (Ger.) stick on stick; stick shot

stone chimes see *lithophone*

stone discs round discs of resonant stone struck by hard *mallets* or *beaters.* Their pitch is determined by the size and thickness. See also *lithophone.*

storm bell cast bronze *bell* with an internal clapper, used to signal alarm or storm warnings

strainer see *snare strainer*

straw fiddle obsolete name for the *xylophone,* so called because the wood *bars* were laid on ropes of straw to increase resonance

street beat see *cadence*

stricknadel (Ger.) knitting needle

string drum single-headed *friction drum* with a cord knotted underneath the head that protrudes out the top. A rosined cloth is pulled along the cord which causes the head to vibrate. Examples include the *dog bark* and *lion's roar.*

strìsciato (It.) to rub; to brush

strohfiedel (Ger.) straw fiddle; xylophone
strung clapper see *bin-sasara*
sturmglocke (Ger.) storm bell
sùghero (It.) cork
sul bórdo (It.) at the edge; at the rim
sulla cassa (It.) on the *drum shell*
sulla corde (It.) snares on
sulla cùpola (It.) on the bell of a cymbal
sulla membrana (It.) on the *drum head*
suòno di bottiglia (It.) tuned bottles
suòno di osso (It.) bones
sur la caisse (Fr.) on the *drum shell*
sur la peau (Fr.) on the *drum head*
sur la protubérance (Fr.) on the bell of a cymbal
sur le bois (Fr.) on the wood
sur le bord (Fr.) at the edge
sur le rebord (Fr.) at the edge
sur les timbres (Fr.) snares on
surdo large metal *tom tom,* played with both beaters and hands, it is the bass voice in Brazilian samba school percussion ensemble
surf effect *sound effect instrument* used to imitate the sound of waves on a beach. A large *frame drum* is turned upside down and small pellets are placed on the head. As the drum is tilted and turned, the pellets slide across the head.
suspended cymbal a *cymbal* that is suspended from a fixed or gooseneck stand. It is used regularly in music for band and orchestra and with a *drum set.*
suspendue (Fr.) suspended
swanee piccolo see *slide whistle*
swanee whistle see *slide whistle*
swish cymbal special effect cymbal; it is a *Chinese cymbal* with rivets installed
Swiss drum see *Basel drum*
switch a bundle of twigs struck against a *drum head* or *drum shell*

T

taballi (It.) timpani
tabèlla (It.) slapstick; clappers

tablā *hand drum* from northern and central India, also known as the dāhinā, it is the higher pitched of the pair of *tablā drums.* It has a wood shell with a single skin head held on with leather straps, which are tightened by sliding small blocks of wood between the strap and the shell. A circular patch of black paste is affixed to the center of the head to help focus the pitch of the drum.

tablā drums in general usage, a pair of *hand drums* common to northern and central India. The higher pitched drum which sets on the player's right is known as the *tablā* or *dāhinā,* and the lower-pitched drum is the *banya* or *duggī.*

tabla trommeln (Ger.) tablā drums

table de bois (Fr.) wooden board

tablettes (Fr.) bones

tabor small drum from the middle ages, used to accompany a pipe whistle. It may have one or two heads and may also have a *snare* across one head. See also *pipe and tabor.*

taiko general term for two-headed, barrel-shaped Japanese drums

tāl general term for small *cymbals* of Southern Asia

taletta (It.) bones

talking drum African drum with an hourglass shell and two heads connected by a single cord laced back and forth between each head. The drum is held under the arm and can be squeezed to tighten the cord, which in turn stretches the head and changes the drum pitch. It is struck with a curved beater.

talking drums any *drum* that is used for communication, which creates sounds that imitate human speech

tam-tam large round metal alloy disc of indefinite pitch. It generally has a flat face and is struck with a large mallet. See also *gong.*

The terms tam-tam and gong are used interchangeably by composers. If the part calls for either instrument (but not both), it probably refers to the large orchestral tam-tam. When the part calls for both instruments, the tam-tam is the larger instrument and the gong the smaller. Gongs may also be notated as having a definite pitch.

tamalin (Af.-Akan) a single-headed rectangular *frame drum* in several different sizes. One hand holds the drum and may press against the inside of the head to mute the tone while the other hand strikes the drum.

tambaque see *atabaqué*

tambor (Por., Sp.) drum
tambor de copa (Sp.) goblet drum
tambor de fricción (Sp.) friction drum
tambor de tronco hendido (Sp.) slit drum
tambor grande (Sp.) bass drum
tambor militar (Sp.) military drum
tambor pequeño (Sp.) snare drum
tambor provenzal (Sp.) tambourin provençal
tambor redoblante (Sp.) tenor drum
tambora (Sp.) bass drum
tamboreto (Sp.) small snare drum
tamboril (Sp.) tabor
tamborilete (Sp.) tambourine
tamborim thin, single-headed *drum* struck with a wooden stick. It is the smallest drum in the Brazilian samba school percussion ensemble.
tamborino (Sp.) tenor drum
tamborón (Sp.) bass drum
tambour (Fr.) snare drum
tambour à corde (Fr.) string drum; lion's roar
tambour à fente (Fr.) slit drum
tambour à friction (Fr.) friction drum
tambour à une seule peau (Fr.) single-headed drum
tambour arabe (Fr.) darabucca
tambour avec timbres (Fr.) snare drum with snares on
tambour con cuerdes (Sp.) string drum
tambour d'acciaio (It.) steel drum
tambour d'acier (Fr.) steel drum
tambour d'empire (Fr.) parade drum
tambour de basque (Fr.) tambourine
tambour de bois (Fr.) slit drum
tambour de frein (Fr.) brake drum
tambour de provence (Fr.) tambourin provençal
tambour en peau de bois (Fr.) wood-plate drum
tambour Indien (Fr.) American Indian drum
tambour militaire (Fr.) military drum
tambour militaire sans timbres (Fr.) military drum without snares
tambour petite (Fr.) small snare drum; piccolo snare drum
tambour provençal (Fr.) tambourin provençal
tambour roulant (Fr.) tenor drum
tambour sur cadre (Fr.) frame drum
tambour tubulaire (Fr.) barrel drum

tambourin (Fr.) a long, narrow, two-headed drum without *snares,* associated with the Provence region in France. Also known as the *tambourin provençal.*
tambourin (Ger.) tambourine
tambourin à main (Fr.) hand drum
tambourin de campagne South American *tambourine*
tambourin de provence see *tambourin*
tambourin provençal (Fr.) originally a small *drum* hung from the wrist to accompany the pipe. The modern instrument is a long, narrow, two-headed drum usually without *snares,* but may also be used with one or two strands of snares.
tambourine a single-headed *frame drum,* with one or two rows of *jingles* or *pellet bells* affixed to the frame. It is struck, shaken, or caused to vibrate by the friction of a *thumb roll* or *finger roll.* The modern rock and pop instrument may not have a head.
tamburelli (It.) tambourines
tamburello (It.) tambourine
tamburello basco (It.) tambourine
tamburetta (It.) tambourine
tamburi baschi (It.) tambourine
tamburi militari (It.) military drums
tamburin (Ger., Rus.) tambourine
tamburin ohne schellen (Ger.) tambourine without jingles; frame drum
tamburino (It., Pol.) tambourine
tamburino senza cimbali (It.) tambourine without jingles; frame drum
tamburinschelle (Ger.) tambourine jingle
tamburo (It.) drum; snare drum
tamburo a calice (It.) goblet drum
tamburo a una pelle (It.) single-headed drum
tamburo acuto (It.) high-pitched drum
tamburo alto (It.) snare drum
tamburo arabo (It.) darabucca
tamburo basco (It.) tambourine
tamburo basco con sonagli (It.) tambourine with jingles
tamburo basso (It.) long drum
tamburo chiaro (It.) snare drum
tamburo d'acciaio (It.) steel drum
tamburo di basilea (It.) parade drum
tamburo di freno (It.) brake drum
tamburo di frizione (It.) friction drum

tamburo di legno (It.) wood block; log drum
tamburo di legno africano (It.) log drum
tamburo di legno pelle (It.) wood-plate drum
tamburo grande (It.) bass drum
tamburo grosso (It.) bass drum
tamburo indiano (It.) American Indian drum
tamburo militaire (It.) military drum
tamburo orientale (It.) Chinese drum
tamburo piccolo (It.) small snare drum; piccolo snare drum
tamburo provenzale (It.) tambourin provençal
tamburo rullante (It.) tenor drum
tamburo senza corde (It.) drum without snares
tamburo sordo South American drum without snares
tamburo tubolare (It.) barrel drum
tamburone (It.) bass drum
tampon (Fr.) double-headed beater
tamtam (Ger.) tam-tam; gong
tanta Latin American gong
tanzkastagnetten (Ger.) dance castanets
tap box wood block
tapan double-headed drum of Eastern Europe
tār *frame drum* of the Middle East
tarbourka see *darabucca*
tarélki (Rus.) cymbals
tarole (Fr.) deep, narrow-diameter *snare drum*
tarolle see *tarole*
tastenxylophon (Ger.) keyboard xylophone
tavola da lavare (It.) washboard
tavola di legno (It.) wooden board
tavolette (It.) wood block; wooden board
taxi horn *sound effect instrument* that imitates an *auto horn*; usually performed by an electric horn or a *bulb horn*

George Gershwin's An American in Paris *calls for four taxi horns tuned to A, B, C, and D. A set of four horns mounted on a frame can be rented from major percussion rental houses for this work.*

tela the thin membrane in the *resonators* of South American and *Mexican marimbas*
teller (Ger.) plates; crash cymbals
tellern (Ger.) plates; crash cymbals
tempelblöcke (Ger.) temple blocks

tempelglocke (Ger.) Japanese temple bell
temple blocks blocks of wood which have been hollowed out to create a large resonating chamber. They were created in the far east and are also known as Korean, Japanese, or Chinese blocks. The wooden blocks may be intricately carved, although modern instruments are also made from moulded plastic.
temple blocs (Fr.) temple blocks
temple cup bell see *Japanese temple bell*
tenabari Latin American *rattles* made from butterfly cocoons
tenor drum a deep, double-headed drum without *snares*

A tenor drum does not have snares; a field or parade drum has snares. There are not definite terms for tenor drum and field drum in the foreign languages. Most foreign composers will notate with or without snares to indicate their preference. The following terms usually refer to a tenor drum: (Ger.) rührtrommel, (It.) cassa rullante, (Fr.) caisse roulante.

Tradition within different orchestras and conductor's preferences will also affect what type of drum is used with the foreign terms.

tenors single-headed *tom toms* mounted in a harness for use in a marching percussion section
tenortrommel (Ger.) tenor drum
tepanahuaste South American *slit drum*
teponaztli Mexican *log drum*
teschio cinese (It.) Chinese wood blocks
tête (Fr.) head; tip
Thai gong a tuned *gong* with a raised *boss* in the center. See also *button gong.*
thumb piano term often used as a generic name for an African *lamellaphone.* Thin metal or wood tongues are fixed on a hollow wood box, which acts as a resonator. The tongues are plucked by the thumbs or fingers, their pitch determined by their length. The instrument is also known by many other names such as *sansa, mbira,* and *kalimba.*
thumb roll method of using friction to sustain sound on a *drum* or *tambourine* by rubbing the thumb across the surface of the head
thunder drum a large, heavy *skin head* attached to a heavy, square, wooden frame. The head is struck with a large *beater.*
thunder sheet a large sheet of tin which is suspended and shaken to imitate the sound of a thunderstorm

thunder stick see *bull roarer*
Tibetan prayer stones see *prayer stones*
tibetanische gebetsteine (Ger.) Tibetan prayer stones
tief (tiefe) (Ger.) low tone; bass note
tiefe glocke (Ger.) low pitched bell
tierschelle (Ger.) cowbell
tierstimmeneffekte (Ger.) animal sound effects
timbal (Sp.) timpani
timbalao *tenor drum* used in Latin America
timbale à pédale (Fr.) pedal timpani
timbales a pair of single-headed, metal shell drums, struck with thin sticks on the heads, rims, and shells. It is used most commonly in Latin American and Cuban music.
timbales (Fr.) timpani
timbales cubaines (Fr.) timbales
timbales cubanis (It.) timbales
timbales cubanos (Sp.) timbales
timbales latino-americano (It.) timbales
timbales orientales (Fr.) tabla drums
timbals (Sp.) timpani
timbrel tambourine; a *frame drum* with *jingles*
timbres (Fr.) 1) jingles or pellet bells; 2) snares on a drum
timbres (Sp.) glockenspiel
timp-toms a set of single-headed tom toms used in the marching percussion section
timpanetti (It.) timbales
timpani tunable drums with a single head of skin or plastic stretched over a bowl-shaped shell of metal or fiberglass. They are tuned by a variety of devices, the modern instruments using a foot pedal system. Both hard and soft beaters are used, and the music is notated in the bass clef. See also *timpano.*
timpani a pedali (It.) pedal timpani
timpani mute a small felt pad placed on the timpani head to reduce resonance
timpani orientali (It.) tablā drums
timpanista (It.) timpanist
timpano a single drum from a set of *timpani*
timpano piccolo (It.) piccolo timpani
timpanos (Sp.) timpani
timpany see *timpani*
timplipito (Rus.) a pair of small, single-headed clay drums with *skin heads* tensioned by leather thongs, tuned approximately a fifth apart

tin horn see *metal rattle*
tin rattle see *metal rattle*
tintements (Fr.) jingles
tintinnarie (It.) jingles
tischglocke (Ger.) dinner bell; hand bell
tlapanhuehuetl Aztec Indian drum
tocsin (Fr.) alarm bell
tôle (Fr.) thunder sheet
tôle pour imiter le tonnerre (Fr.) thunder sheet
tom tom single or double-headed drum of varying depth and diameter. They are used as part of a *drum set,* or as *concert tom toms.*
tom tom à una pelle (It.) single-headed *tom tom*
tom tom aigu (Fr.) high-pitched *tom tom*
tom tom chinois (Fr.) Chinese tom tom
tom tom cinese (It.) Chinese tom tom
tom tom grave (Fr.) large tom tom
tom tom spiel (Ger.) roto toms
tonnerre à poignée (Fr.) thunder sheet
tontrommel (Ger.) small drum with a clay shell
top cymbal see *ride cymbal*
totodzi (Af.-Ewe) a small, single-headed, wooden *drum,* played with wooden sticks
toy drum a small *drum* of narrow width and depth, intended for use as a child's toy
tr. abbreviation for *tremolo*
traditional grip a manner of holding *drum sticks* developed for playing a drum slung around the neck which hangs at an angle. The right hand holds the stick between the thumb and index finger with the palm down; the left hand is held with the stick resting in the web between the thumb and index finger and supported by the third and fourth fingers with the wrist in a vertical position.
train whistle *sound effect instrument* with two or three pipes of different pitch blown from a single mouthpiece, used to imitate a steam engine whistle
trap set see *drum set*
traps a generic term for small percussion and effects instruments, generally associated with early theater, vaudeville, and film percussionists
tremolo in percussion music, an indication to play a *roll* or a sustained sound on the instrument. It often appears over the note abbreviated as "tr."

trepei (Fr.) triangle
treppiede (It.) triangle
treschotka (Rus.) ratchet; cog rattle
trezvonï (Rus.) chimes
triangel (Ger.) triangle
triangelschlägel gestrichen (Ger.) scrape with a triangle beater
triangelschlegel (Ger.) triangle beater
triangle a length of steel rod bent into the shape of a triangle which rings with a sustained tone of indefinite pitch. The instrument is suspended and struck with a small metal *beater.*
triàngolo (It.) triangle
tríangulo (Sp.) triangle
trill colle monete (It.) roll with coins
triller (Ger.) trill; shake
triller avec des pièces de monnaie (Fr.) roll with coins
trillerpfeife (Ger.) alarm whistle; pea whistle
trillo (It.) tremolo; shake
trinidad-gongtrommel (Ger.) steel drum
trinquete (Sp.) ratchet
trocano large log drum
trogxylophon (Ger.) trough xylophone
trolées (Fr.) tremolo
tromme (Dan.) drum
trommel (Dut., Ger.) drum
trommelfell (Ger.) drum head
trommeln (Ger.) drum
trommelreifen (Ger.) counter hoop
trommelschlegel (Ger.) drum sticks
trommelstocken (Ger.) drum sticks
trommelwirbel (Ger.) drum roll
trompe d'auto (Fr.) auto horn
trompe de brume (Fr.) fog horn
troncs d'arbres (Fr.) log drum
trough xylophone xylophone *bars* set over a box, or trough, often used in *gamelan* ensembles. The trough acts as a *resonator* for all *bars* on the instrument.
tubalcain keyboard glockenspiel
tubaphon (Ger.) tubaphone
tubaphone a *mallet percussion instrument* with steel or brass tubes, rather than *bars*
tubaphono (It.) tubaphone
tube bells chimes

tube shaker metal tube filled with pellets or seeds, also known as *chocalho*

tubes de bambou (Fr.) bamboo wind chimes

tubes de cloches (Fr.) chimes

tubi di bambù (It.) bamboo wind chimes

tubo metal shaker

tubo sonoro (It.) tube shaker

tubofono (It.) tubaphone

tubs slang term for *drums* or the *drum set*

tubular bells see *chimes*

tubular chimes see *chimes*

tubular wood block a cylindrical *wood block* with slits in either end, making it capable of two tones

tubuscampanophon (Ger.) tubaphone

tumba the largest size of *conga drum*

tumbadora (Ger.) tumba; African drum

tun Central American *slit drum*

tuned bottles glass bottles, arranged by pitch, to create a diatonic or chromatic scale. They are suspended from a rack and played as a *mallet percussion instrument.* The pitch of the bottle is determined by its size and thickness, and can be fine-tuned by adding water inside the vessel.

tuned glasses water glasses, tuned to pitch by adding water inside the vessel, usually struck by *mallets*

tuneful percussion pitched *mallet percussion instruments,* such as the *xylophone, glockenspiel, hand bells,* and *chimes,* called for in music by Percy Grainger

tuoni (It.) thunder sheet

tuòno a pugno (It.) thunder sheet

tupan double-headed, wooden drum with *skin heads,* common to Yugoslavia and Bulgaria

Türkische becken (Ger.) Turkish cymbals

Türkische musik (Ger.) Janissary music

Turkish crescent a metal staff or stick adorned with *pellet bells* and cup bells, sometimes topped with a crescent moon. Also known as a *jingling Johnny,* it is used in *Janissary music,* where it is shaken and rhythmically pounded on the ground.

Turkish drum a double-headed *bass drum,* used in Turkish bands through the 18th century

turmglockenspiel (Ger.) carillon bells; chimes

tuyau de fer (Fr.) iron pipe

two plate roll sustained sound on *crash cymbals* created by short, rapid strokes of the cymbals against each other
tympali (Ger.) timpani
tympani see *timpani*
tympano see *timpano*
tympany see *timpani*
tympelles (Ger.) timpani
typewriter an actual office typewriter used as a *sound effect instrument*

❧ U

uccelli (It.) bird whistle
udar (Rus.) percussion
udárnye instruménty (Rus.) percussion instruments
uder (Cze.) percussion
umstimmen (Ger.) to change the tuning; to retune
una-fon small electronic keyboard instrument manufactured by the J. C. Deagan Company in the 1930s
ùnghia (It.) fingernail
unterreifen (Ger.) flesh hoop
usignuolo (It.) nightingale bird call
üstdob (Hun.) timpani

❧ V

vasentrommel (Ger.) goblet drum
velare (It.) to mute; to muffle; to choke
vérga (It.) wire brushes
verge (Fr.) wire brushes

Although this term translates as "switch," most performers will use a set of wire brushes. We usually find this term with regard to snare drum parts, it should not be confused with the German term "rute" which refers to a bundle of twigs played on the bass drum head or shell.

verghe (It.) wire brushes
verhallen (Ger.) dying away
verklingen lassen (Ger.) let vibrate; don't dampen; allow the sound to die away
verres choqués (Fr.) glass harmonica; glass harp
verrillon (Fr.) musical glasses
verstärkungsröhre (Ger.) resonators
verstimmung (Ger.) out of tune
vessel rattle a hollow container of gourd, wood, or metal filled with sand or shot. Examples include *chocalho* and *maracas.*
vetrata (It.) sandpaper blocks
vibes common term for *vibraphone*
vibrafón (Rus.) vibraphone
vibrafoni (It.) vibraphone
vibrafono (It.) vibraphone
vibraharp brand name used by the J. C. Deagan Company for their models of the *vibraphone*
vibraphon (Ger.) vibraphone
vibraphone *mallet percussion instrument* developed in the United States in the 1920s. The *bars* are metal or aluminum alloy with a typical range of three octaves. A damper pad touches each bar and is attached to a foot-operated pedal, to control note duration and phrasing. A small disc sits at the top of each *resonator* and is connected to an electric motor. As the discs rotate, they break up the air column, giving the instrument's tone a vibrato quality. The instrument sounds at written pitch.
vibraphone (without fans) play the instrument with the motor turned off; without vibrato effect
vibraphonschlägel (Ger.) vibraphone mallet
vibraphonspieler (Ger.) vibraphonist
vibraslap rattling instrument, the modern version of the *jawbone of an ass.* A small wooden box holding metal pins is attached by a bent steel rod to a wooden ball. When the ball is struck or slapped, the pins vibrate and rattle inside the box.
viehschelle (Ger.) cowbell
Viennese cymbals medium-heavy *crash cymbals,* generally used with 19th-century Viennese orchestral literature
vogelgesang (Ger.) bird song; nightingale bird call
vogelpfeife (Ger.) bird call
vogelruf (Ger.) bird call
voilé (voilée) (Fr.) muted; *muffled*
vorschlag (Ger.) grace note; ornament

W

wachtel (Ger.) quail bird call

wachtelpfeife (Ger.) quail bird call

waldteufel small *friction drum* with a single *skin head.* A cord is tied under the head and is looped around a small stick. As the *drum shell* is spun in the air, the head vibrates with a buzzing sound.

walzentrommel (Ger.) cylindrical drum

wasamba rattle African *rattle* made from an L-shaped tree branch. One fork serves as a handle, while dried fruit husks are suspended from the other fork. As the instrument is shaken, the husks clatter together.

wasamba-rassel (Ger.) wasamba rattle

waschbrett (Ger.) washboard

washboard a household laundry washboard with a wood frame and corrugated metal surface. The metal surface is scraped with a wood or metal stick or by fingertips covered by metal sewing thimbles.

water buffalo bells see *herd bells*

water chimes metal *chimes* which are struck to sound their tone, then lowered into a container filled with water. This gives the effect of a *glissando,* "bending" the tone and lowering the pitch of the chime.

water drum *American Indian drum* with a single-head and a vessel body that is filled with water. The amount of water affects the tuning of the drum. The body may be wood, clay, or metal, and the instrument is struck with hands, gourds, or beaters.

water gong a *gong* which is struck, then lowered into a container filled with water. This gives the effect of a *glissando,* "bending" the tone and lowering the pitch of the instrument.

water gourd a half-section of a hollow gourd which floats upside down in a container of water. The gourd is struck with a wooden spoon or small stick.

waterphone a sound sculpture consisting of a hollow metal container filled with water and a *resonator* tube extending up from the center of the container. Brass rods of different lengths and thicknesses are welded around the circumference of the container. The rods are struck, plucked, or bowed as the instrument is turned, causing the water inside to move and changing the pitch of the note by a *glissando* effect.

wechseln (Ger.) to change
wechseln in (Ger.) change to; used in *timpani* music to notate a change of pitch
weich (Ger.) soft
weiche schlägel (Ger.) soft sticks; soft-headed mallets
weicher filz (Ger.) soft felt
wellensirene (Ger.) siren
werbel (Pol.) drum roll
whip *sound effect instrument* used to imitate a whip crack, usually made by a *slapstick*
whirled friction drum small *friction drum* with a single *skin head.* A cord is tied under the head and is looped around a small stick. As the *drum shell* is spun in the air, the head vibrates with a buzzing sound.
whistle *sound effect instrument* played by blowing air across or through a tube. The shape and material of the whistle affects the tone, although it tends to sound a constant pitch. Examples include the *bosun's pipe, police whistle, nightingale bird call,* and *siren whistle.*
whizzer see *whirled friction drum*
wickelreifen (Ger.) flesh hoop
wiege (Ger.) trough xylophone
wind chimes small pieces of glass, wood, or metal which are suspended individually from a frame. They give a tinkling sound when they brush against each other.
wind machine a large cylinder made of wooden slats which is set on a stand and covered by canvas, denim, or heavy cloth. A hand-crank turns the cylinder which rotates under the cloth to imitate the sound of wind blowing.
windglocken (Ger.) wind chimes
windmaschine (Ger.) wind machine
wine glass a crystal glass which is rubbed around the rim with a moistened finger. It sounds an ethereal, high-pitched tone, the pitch of which can be altered by adding water to the glass.
wirbel (Ger.) drum roll
wirbel mit den fingern (Ger.) finger roll
wirbeltrommel (Ger.) tenor drum
wire brushes a type of *drum stick* consisting of lengths of thin wire spread in a fan shape and set into a handle. They are often used for soft playing on a *drum set.*
wolle (Ger.) wool
wollschlägel (Ger.) wool-headed stick

wood and straw instrument obsolete term for the *xylophone*

wood bell a *bell* made from part of a tree trunk that has been hollowed out and fitted with an internal clapper

wood block small block of hard wood with a resonating chamber cut in the side. It may be rectangular or tubular in shape and are struck with wood sticks or hard rubber *mallets.*

wood drum see *slit drum* or *log drum*

wood pile slang term for the *xylophone*

wood-plate drum a *drum* with a wood head. It may be constructed by covering a regular *tom tom* with a wooden lid or plate.

wooden barrel see *sake barrel*

wooden board oblong wooden board struck with a wooden *mallet* or *hammer.* See also *sēmantron.*

wooden clapper see *slapstick*

wooden fish see *temple blocks*

wooden scraper see *reco-reco*

wooden tom tom see *wood-plate drum*

X

xaque-xaque Brazilian rattle

xilofón (Sp.) xylophone

xilofón bajo (Sp.) bass xylophone

xilofono (It.) xylophone

xilofóno (Sp.) xylophone

xilofono a tastiera (It.) keyboard xylophone

xilofono basso (It.) bass xylophone

xilofono in cassetta di risonanza (It.) trough xylophone

xilomarimba (It.) xylomarimba

xilorgano (Sp.) xylophone

xucalho (Braz.) metal shaker, similar to the *chocalho*

xylofon (Cze., Dan., Swe) xylophone

xylomarimba see *xylorimba*

xylophon (Ger.) xylophone

xylophone *mallet percussion instrument* with tuned *bars* of wood or synthetic material. The instrument can trace its history in Africa, Asia, South America, and Europe through various forms of construction. The instrument was built in a variety of sizes, with the modern concert instrument 3 $^1/_2$ octaves in range and sounding one octave above written pitch.

xylophone à cassette-résonance (Fr.) trough xylophone

xylophone à clavier (Fr.) keyboard xylophone

xylophone, alto see *alto xylophone*

xylophone, alto-soprano see *alto-soprano xylophone*

xylophone basse (Fr.) bass xylophone

xylophone, soprano see *soprano xylophone*

xylophonschlegel (Ger.) xylophone mallet

xylorimba *mallet percussion instrument* with an extended range to encompass the low notes of the *marimba* and the high notes of the *xylophone.* They were manufactured in the 1920s and 1930s to combine the sound characteristics and range of both instruments.

xylosistron friction instrument consisting of a set of horizontal wood bars that are stroked by the player who wears rosined gloves

Y

yuka cylindrical, single-headed Afro-Cuban drum, constructed in three sizes, similar to a *conga drum*

yunque (Sp.) anvil

Z

zabumba (Braz.) bass drum

zacapa Bolivian jingle rattle

zambomba *friction drum* of Spain and Central and South America

zambumba snare drum of El Salvador

zanza see *sansa*

zapotecano *Mexican marimba* with gourd *resonators*

zarge (Ger.) drum shell

ziehpfeife (Ger.) slide whistle

ziemlich hart (Ger.) medium hard

ziemlich weich (Ger.) medium soft

zilafono (It.) xylophone
zilofono (It.) xylophone
zils *finger cymbals,* played like *castanets,* used in ancient and modern Islamic music
zimbel (Ger.) cymbal
zimbeln (Ger.) cymbals; also *antique cymbals* or *crotales*
zinger cymbal a small *cymbal* mounted to the *rim* of a *bass drum* and struck by a *cymbal striker* attached to a *bass drum beater*
zischend (Ger.) hissing; instruction to draw a metal beater or a coin across the edge of a *cymbal.* It may also be played with a pair of *crash cymbals,* sliding the top edge of one cymbal against the inside of the other.

Whenever a composer uses this term or the English word "swish" for cymbals, the above technique is used. Orchestral players will also use this technique for very soft cymbal strokes even without an indication by the composer. This is strictly an interpretive call by the player or conductor.

zu 2 (Ger.) with two players or two instruments

This term is common in Mahler's music and specifically means to use more than one player on the part. Do not confuse this term with the use of "à2" for crash cymbals.

zumbador (Sp.) friction drum
zurriago (Sp.) whip; slapstick
zurückstimmen (Ger.) retune
zusammenschlagen (Ger.) to crash (cymbals) together
zuzá see *chocalho*
zweifacher vorschlag (Ger.) drag
zweifelltrommel (Ger.) double-headed drum
zylindertrommel (Ger.) cylindrical drum
zymbal (Ger.) small cymbal
zymbel (Ger.) cymbal

~ PHRASES

What follows is a list of phrases found in the standard orchestral literature, arranged alphabetically by composer, composition, instrument, and the first word of the phrase. Each is given as it appears in the published music, followed by its language abbreviation, the English translation of the phrase, and the instrumental part in which it is notated.

BARTÓK: CONCERTO NO. 2 FOR PIANO

- **Tamburo Piccolo**

Abwärtsgestrichene Noten sind immer am Rand, aufwärtsgestrichene in der Mitte des Fells zu spielen.
(Ger.) Play notes with the stems down at the edge of the drum head; play notes with stems up in the center of the drum head.

- **Triangolo**

Alle Noten sind mit einem Holzstäbchen zu spielen, ausgenommen die mit + bezeichneten, welche mit einem Metallstäbchen zu spielen sind.
(Ger.) Play all notes with a wood stick, except those marked with +, which are to be played with a metal stick.

BARTÓK: CONCERTO FOR VIOLIN

- **Cymbal**

Avec la lame d'un canif sur le bord.
(Fr.) With blade of a penknife on the edge [of the cymbal].

Baguettes en bois, avec l'extrémité grosse, sur la bord de la cymbale.
(Fr.) To be played with the thick end of a wood stick on the edge of the cymbal.

Baguettes en bois, avec l'extrémité mince, sur la protubérance du milieu.
(Fr.) To be played with the thin end of a wood stick on the dome of the cymbal.

- **Snare Drum**

Au bord de la membrane.
(Fr.) At the edge of the drum head.

La note sous la ligne sera exécutée au bord de la membrane.
(Fr.) The notes below the line are to be played at the edge of the drum head.

- **Timpani**

Baguettes de caisse claire, sur le bord de la membrane.
(Fr.) With side drum sticks, at the edge of the head.

Baguettes en bois, à être éxécuté sur le bord de la membrane.
(Fr.) With wood sticks, to be played at the edge of the drum head.

Le joueur de la caisse claire ou de la grosse caisse.
(Fr.) [To be played by the] snare drummer or bass drummer.

BARTÓK: *THE MIRACULOUS MANDARIN*

- **Gran Cassa**

Bei den mit rechten Hand gespielten Noten der Oberstimme soll das Fell mit dem Griff eines Kleinen Trommelschlägels berührt werden.
(Ger.) Play notes with the stems up with the right hand, striking the head with the handle of a drum stick.

Bei der mit der rechten Hand gespielten Oberstimme soll des Fell mit dem Holzschaft eines Paukenschlägels berührt werden.
(Ger.) Play the notes that are stems up with the right hand, striking the head with the wood handle of the timpani mallet.

- **Tamburo Grande**

Die Unterstimme mit der linken, die Oberstimme mit der rechten Hand zu spielen; die linke Hand benützt bis [69] einen biegsamen Stab, mit dessen oberer Hälfte das Fell berührt wird.
(Ger.) Play the notes with the stems down with the left hand and the notes with the stems up with the right hand; From this point until rehearsal no. 69, the left hand uses a stick with a flexible shaft, striking the drum head with the upper half of the shaft.

BARTÓK: MUSIC FOR STRING INSTRUMENTS, PERCUSSION AND CELESTA

- **Snare Drum**

Am Rand des Felles.
(Ger.) Played at the edge of the drum head.

Von hier an in der Mitte des Felles.
(Ger.) From this point, play in the center of the head.

- **Cymbals**

Kleineres Instrument mit höherem Ton.
(Ger.) Use a smaller instrument with a higher pitch.

BERLIOZ: SYMPHONIE FANTASTIQUE

- **Campane**

A défaut de Cloches derrière le Théâtre plusieurs Pianos sur l'avant scène.
(Fr.) In the absence of bells back stage, play with several pianos on the apron.

Derrière la Scène.
(Fr.) [Played] behind the scene. [Played backstage.]

Wenn keine Glocken hinter der Scene vorhanden sind, mehrere Klaviere im Vordergrund der Scene.
(Ger.) In the absence of bells back stage, play with several pianos on the apron.

- **Cinelli**

Frappez un coup avec une baguette converte d'éponge sur une des cymbales.
(Fr.) Strike the cymbal with a sponge-headed drum stick.

- **Gran Tamburo**

Étouffez le son avec la main.
(Fr.) Dampen the tone with the hand.

Deux Timbaliers (3me et 4me) avec des baguettes d'éponge.
(Fr.) The third and fourth timpanists should play [the bass drum] using sponge-headed drum sticks.

Grosse-Caisse placée debout et employée comme timbale.
(Fr.) The bass drum should be placed upright and played like a timpani.

Roulante jouée par 2 Timbaliers.
(Fr.) [The bass drum] roll is to be played by two timpanists [with timpani sticks].

- **Timpani I**

Die erste Achtelnote jedes halben Taktes wird mit zwei Schlägeln geschlagen, die andern fünf Achtelnoten mit dem Schlägel der rechten Hand.
(Ger.) The first eighth note of each half measure is to be played with both sticks; the other five eighth notes with the right hand stick.

La première croche de chaque demi-mesure avec deux baguettes, et les cinq autres croches avec la baguette de la main droite.
(Fr.) The first eighth note of each half measure is to be played with both sticks; the other five eighth notes with the right hand stick.

Tout les Timbaliers baguettes d'éponge.
(Fr.) All [four] timpanists should use sponge-headed mallets.

CHABRIER: *ESPAÑA*

- **Grosse Caisse et Cymbales**

Une Cymbale suspendue par sa courroie roulement avec deux baguette d'éponge.
(Fr.) Roll with sponge [soft] mallets on one cymbal suspended by its strap. [i.e., a suspended cymbal]

DUKAS: *LA PERI*

- **Cymbales**

En effleurant à peine les deux plateaux.
(Fr.) Gently touch the two cymbals together.

Laissez vibrer doucement en effleurant à peine les deux plateaux.
(Fr.) Let vibrate by gently allowing the two cymbals to barely touch together.

Roulement avec deux Baguettes de Timbales.
(Fr.) Roll with two timpani mallets.

DUKAS: *L'APPRENTI SORCIER*

- **Cymbales**

Les roulements indiqués à la partie de cymbales doivent être exécutés avec deux baguettes de timbales sur l'un des planteaux de l'instrument suspendu par sa courroie. Les roulements de Grosse Caisse avec une double mailloche.
(Fr.) The rolls indicated on the cymbal part should be played using two timpani mallets [i.e. soft mallets] on a suspended cymbal. The rolls on the bass drum should be played using a double-headed mallet.

MAHLER: SYMPHONY NO. 1

- **Grosse Trommel**

  Die Becken sind an dieser Stelle an der Grosse Trommel anzuhängen. Becken und Trommelstimme sind von einem und demselben Musiker zu schlagen.
  (Ger.) The cymbals are to be attached to the bass drum. Both instruments are to be played by the same musician.

- **Timpani I**

  Dämpfung ab.
  (Ger.) Remove muffler.

MAHLER: SYMPHONY NO. 2

- **Timpani I**

  I. benützt die kleine Pauke des II. Spielers.
  (Ger.) Player One uses the small timpani of Player Two.

  I. nimmt die As-Pauke des II. Spielers zur Benützung dieser Stelle.
  (Ger.) Player One uses Player Two's A♭ timpani at this place.

  Kurz. jeden Ton abdämpfen.
  (Ger.) Briefly dampen each tone.

- **Kleine Trommel**

  Mehrere kleine Trommeln.
  (Ger.) [Use] several snare drums.

- **Tiefe Glocken**

  Tiefe Glocken von unbestimmten Klang.
  (Ger.) Low-tone bells of indefinite pitch.

MAHLER: SYMPHONY NO. 3

- **Grosse Trommel, Triangel, Ruthe, Tam-tam**

Becken an der grossen Trommel befestigt, aber ohne grosse Trommel.
(Ger.) [Play the] cymbal attached to the bass drum, but without the bass drum. [i.e., cymbal alone]

Becken angebunden aber von einem 2. Musiker geschlagen.
(Ger.) The cymbal [attached to the bass drum] is played by two players.

Von Einem geschlagen.
(Ger.) [The bass drum and cymbal are to be] struck by one player.

- **Kleine Trommel**

Kleine Trommel (in der Entfernung aufgestellt).
(Ger.) Snare drum (placed at a distance). [offstage]

MAHLER: SYMPHONY NO. 4

- **Becken**

Becken mit Schwammschlägel klingen lassen.
(Ger.) Strike the suspended cymbal with soft mallets and let the cymbal vibrate. [Do not muffle the tone.]

- **Pauke**

Mit 2 Schlägeln.
(Ger.) With 2 mallets. [Strike the drum head with both mallets simultaneously.]

MAHLER: SYMPHONY NO. 5

- **Pauke**

Gewöhnliche Schlägel.
(Ger.) Use the normal sticks.

Holzschlägel (immer abdämpfen).
(Ger.) With wood mallets (always dampened).

- **Tamtam**

Immer klingen lassen.
(Ger.) Always let the instrument vibrate. [Do not dampen the tone.]

MAHLER: SYMPHONY NO. 6

- **Grosse Trommel**

Mit einem Holzstäbchen auf dem Holzrand der Trommel geschlagen.
(Ger.) Strike the wooden rim of the drum with a wood stick.

Zussammenraffen von Becken und Trommel.
(Ger.) Quickly take up cymbals and bass drum.

- **Hammer**

Becken und Tam-Tam nur im Falle der Hammer nicht ausreichend besetzt ist.
(Ger.) Cymbals and tam-tam should play only if the hammer is not sufficiently penetrating.

Kurzer, mächtig, aber dumpf hallender Schlag von nicht metallischem Charakter (wie ein Axthieb).
(Ger.) A short, power, but dull resounding tone (like an axe blow), but not of a metallic character.

- **Herdenglocken**

Herdenglocken im Orchester.
(Ger.) Herd bells [almglocken] played in the orchestra.

Herdenglocken in der Ferne.
(Ger.) Herd bells [almglocken] played in the distance [offstage].

- **Kleine Trommel**

Kleine Trommel doppelt besetzt.
(Ger.) Double the snare drum part.

- **Rute**

Rute (auf Holz).
(Ger.) Strike the rute on the wood shell of the drum.

- **Tiefes Glockengeläute**

Tiefes Glockenspiel in der Ferne.
(Ger.) Low tone bell played in the distance [offstage].

Zwei oder mehrere sehr teife Glocken von unbestimmten aber von einander verschiedenen Klang, in der Ferne aufgestellt und leise und unregelmässig geschlagen.
(Ger.) Two or more very low tone bells of indefinite pitch, but of different pitches, set up in the distance and quietly and irregularly struck.

MAHLER: SYMPHONY NO. 7

- **Glockenspiel**

Mit beiden Händen.
(Ger.) with both hands.

Mit Klöppeln.
(Ger.) [Glockenspiel played] with mallets.

- **Grosse Trommel**

In der rechten Hand eine Rute, in der linken einen Schwammschlägel.
(Ger.) In the right hand, hold the rute; in the left hand hold a soft mallet.

- **Herdenglocken**

Herdenglocken sind immer discret und intermittierend in realistischer Nachahmung des Glockengebimmeln einer weidenden Herde zu spielen.
(Ger.) Herd bells are to be always played discreetly and intermittently in realistic imitation of the jingling bells of a feasting herd.

- **Pauken**

Achtung auf dem Wechsel der betonten und unbetonten Noten.
(Ger.) Make a distinction between the stressed and unstressed notes.

MAHLER: SYMPHONY NO. 9

- **Pauken**

Vier Pauken für zwei Spieler; zwei hohe, zwei tiefe Pauken. Die kleinere hohe huß den Umfant [bass clef notes C and A-flat] haben.
(Ger.) Four timpani for two players; two high and two low drums. The smaller drum has the notes C and A-flat.

MASSENET: *LE CID*

- **Triangle et Tambour de Basque**

Les deux exécutants chargés des parties de Grande Caisse et Cymbales prendront pour ce morceau le Triangle et le Tambour de Basque (à défaut de deux exécutants, jouer de préférence la partie de Tambour de Basque).
(Fr.) The two players playing the bass drum and cymbal parts will, in this movement, play the triangle and tambourine parts (in the absence of two players to play the tambourine part).

Les exécutants chargés de la partie Grande Caisse et Cymbales prendront chacun un Tambour de Basque (à défaut) un seul Tambour de Basque.
(Fr.) The two players playing the bass drum and cymbal parts will each play the tambourine part, or (failing this), only one will play the tambourine part.

Reprendre la Grande Caisse et Cymbales.
(Fr.) Return to the bass drum and cymbal parts.

MILHAUD: *LA CRÉATION DU MONDE*

- **Batterie**

La partie de Batterie peut ètre éxécutée par un seul

instrumentiste, à condition d'employer une G.C, à pied [Grosse Caisse à Pied] avec Cymb. décrochable.
(Fr.) The percussion part can be played by only one instrumentalist, on the condition that they use a bass drum with a foot pedal and a detachable cymbal striker.

- **Caisse claire**

Appuyer une baguette sur la peau et frapper sur cette baguette avec l'autre.
(Fr.) Rest one stick on the drum head and strike it with the other. [i.e., stick shot]

- **Grosse caisse**

Accrochez la cymbale à la pédale.
(Fr.) Reconnect the cymbal [or cymbal striker] attached to the bass drum pedal.

Avec baguette de bois (á la main).
(Fr.) [Strike the cymbal] with wood stick (with the hand). [i.e., not played with the metal cymbal striker.]

Décrochez la cymbale.
(Fr.) Unhook the cymbal. [Play with bass drum alone with no cymbal striker.]

- **Tambour de basque**

Le trille indique le pouce, l'accent le coup frappé avec le poing.
(Fr.) The trill is played by a thumb roll, with the accented blow struck with the fist.

STRAUSS: SALOME'S DANCE

- **Timpani**

Wenn keine pedalpauken vorhanden, nur die nicht eingeklammerten noten spielen.
(Ger.) If a pedal timpani is not available, play only the notes in parentheses.

STRAVINSKY: *HISTOIRE DU SOLDAT*

2 Caisses claires sans timbre de taille différante. [grande taille, petite taille]
(Fr.) 2 snare drums of different sizes, both without snares. [large size, small size]

Au milieu de la membrane; au bord de la membrane.
(Fr.) [Strike the bass drum] in the middle of the head; at the edge of the head.

Comme plus haut, au bord et au milieu de la membrane.
(Fr.) [Strike the bass drum] as before, in the middle and at the edge of the head.

Les queues en haut pour la main droite, les queues en bas pour la main gauche.
(Fr.) Play the notes with stems up with the right hand; play the notes with stems down with the left hand.

Tenir dans la main droite une baguette en jonc à tête en capoc et se servir de celle-ci pour frapper le tambour de basque et la caisse claire; dans la main gauche - la mailloche pour frapper la grosse caisse.
(Fr.) In the right hand, hold a cane stick with a fiber tip to strike the tambourine and the large snare drum [without snares]. In the left hand, hold a mallet with a leather head to strike the bass drum.

STRAVINSKY: *LE SACRE DU PRINTEMPS*

- **Tam-tam**

Glissez rapidement avec la baquuette de triangle décrivant un arc sur la surfàce d' l'instrument.
(Fr.) Quickly scrape the triangle beater in an arc across the surface of the instrument.

- **Timpani**

La croche ne change pas de valeur.
(Fr.) The eighth note does not change its value. [i.e., the eighth note beat remains constant.]

ABOUT THE AUTHOR

Russ Girsberger holds degrees in music education, music history, and library and information science. He served as Assistant Chief Librarian with the United States Marine Band in Washington, D.C., and was the first to hold the position of Librarian with the Percussive Arts Society. Currently he is Performance Librarian for the New England Conservatory in Boston, Massachusetts. Girsberger is a member of the Major Orchestra Librarians Association (MOLA) and the Music Library Association.

ABOUT THE EDITOR

Anthony J. Cirone received his Bachelor of Science and Master of Science degrees from the Juilliard School of Music where he studied with Saul Goodman, solo timpanist of the New York Philharmonic.

He is currently Professor of Music at San José State University where he heads the Percussion Department and also teaches the Manuscript Preparation/Computer Engraving section of the Music Technology course. Cirone has also been on the faculty of San Francisco State University and Stanford University.

He is the Percussion Consultant/Editor for Warner Bros. Publishing Company, and is the author of *Portraits in Rhythm,* a collection of 50 studies for snare drum, used worldwide as a standard text for training percussionists in colleges and universities. Anthony Cirone is an active clinician for the Avedis Zildjian Cymbal Company.